Lonni Collins Pratt
Father Daniel Homan, O.S.B.

Here I Am, Lord 2

A Prayer Journal for Teens

Our Sunday Visitor Publishing Division
Our Sunday Visitor, Inc.
Huntington, Indiana 46750

The authors and publisher are grateful to all copyright holders, who are listed in the Acknowledgments and elsewhere, without whose material this work could not have been completed. With the exception of minor changes for stylistic consistency and similar considerations, the excerpted matter appears as originally published. Most if not all of the scriptural citations in this work are from the *New International Version of the Bible*, © 1985 by, and used by permission of, The Zondervan Corporation, Grand Rapids, Mich. Every effort has been made to cite all original sources and secure permissions as needed. If any copyrighted materials have been inadvertently used in this work without proper credit being given in one manner or another, please notify Our Sunday Visitor in writing so that future printings of this work may be corrected accordingly.

International Standard Book Number: 0-87973-705-0
Library of Congress Catalog Card Number: 00-130353

Cover design and layout by Tyler Ottinger
Cover photo © Stockbyte

PRINTED IN THE UNITED STATES OF AMERICA

For Father Michael Green

Acknowledgments

Excerpted or adapted materials appearing in this work are preceded by the chapters (sessions) in which they appear.

3 / What Awesome Really Means — Adapted from *The Annie Dillard Reader* by Annie Dillard, pp. 15-17; Harper Perennial, 1994.

4 / What Kind of Power Does God Have? — From *The Jesus I Never Knew* by Philip Yancey, Zondervan, 1995.

7 / What Do People Need? —From *Seasons of the Heart* by John Powell; originally from the video *Free to Be Me,* Tabor Publishing, 1987.

10 / Shivering Magic — From *Credo* by Brian Doyle, pp. 15-16, St. Mary's Press, 1999.

11 / The Way Home — From *Traveling Mercies* by Anne LaMott, pp. 54-55, Pantheon, Random House, 1999.

12 / Questionable Evidence —From *Front Porch Tales* by Philip Gulley, pp. 49-51, Multnomah, 1997.

16 / Desert Graffiti —Excerpt from *In the Desert We Do Not Count the Days* (pp. 73-75), Holy Cow! Press, 1991; copyright © 1991 by John Brandi; reprinted by permission of the publisher.

17 / Humble Like a Sparrow — From *Humility: 31 Reflections on Christian Virtue* by Robert F. Morneau, p. 19, St. Mary's Press, 1997.

18 / Growing Pains — From *Beach Combing at Miramar: The Quest for an Authentic Life* by Richard Bode, Warner Books, 1997.

19 / First Class All the Way to the Wrong Place — From *Don't Jump to Conclusions Without a Bungee Cord and Other Wise Advice: Devotions for Teens From the Book of Proverbs* by Martha Bolton, Servant Publications, 1999.

20 / Afraid of the Big Bad Wolf — Adapted from *Morning Sun on a White Piano: Simple Pleasures and the Sacramental Life* by Dr. Robin R. Meyers, pp. 70-72, Doubleday, 1998.

22 / Living in the Land of Violence — From *Front Porch Tales* by Philip Gulley, pp. 101-102, Multnomah, 1997.

23 / What My Heart Already Knows — From *My Heart Already Knows* by Rick Elias, Mark Robertson, and Rich Mullins; permission received from Careers-BMG Music Publishing, Inc., © 1999 Careers-BMG Music Publishing Inc. (BMI), Alien Autopsy (SESAC), and Liturgy Legacy Music/Word Music, Inc. (ASCAP); also from "Kallet's Column," by Herbert I. Kallet, M.D.; compiled and reprinted from *Bulletin*, pp. 22-24, Sinai Hospital of Detroit.

25 / Loving Like Ethel — From *A Perfect Storm* by Sebastian Junger, Harper Collins, 1998.

26 / Chicken Soup for the Soul Is Not Enough — From an article by George Carlin in *Free Inquiry*, Summer, 1999.

27 / What Arthur Miller Wanted to Tell Marilyn Monroe — From *Finding Happiness in the Most Unlikely Places* by Donald McCullough; permission granted by Dr. Donald W. McCullough.

35 / The Question Is Why — Adapted from *Children Are Images of Grace: A Pediatrician's Trilogy of Faith, Hope and Love* by Diane M. Komp, M.D., p. 67, Harper Collins/Zondervan, 1996.

36 / Living with a Conscience — From *A Walk in the Woods* by Bill Bryson, copyright © 1997 by Bill Bryson; used by permission of Broadway Books, a division of Random House.

37 / Better Than You Know — From *Letters from Side Lake: A Chronicle of Life in the North Woods* by Peter M. Leschak, pp. 48-49, University of Minnesota Press, Minneapolis; 1992 (an earlier hardcover was published by Harper & Row in 1987); permission received from University of Minnesota Press, copyright 1992 by Peter M. Leschak.

39 / Good Advice — Max Ehrmann; copyright 1927 by Max Ehrmann, copyright renewed 1954 by Bertha K. Ehrmann, reprinted by permission, Robert L. Bell, Melrose, MA 02176.

41 / I'm Only Human (Not That There's Anything Wrong with That) — From *Beloved* by Toni Morrison, pp. 88-89, Picador, 1996.

42 / Star Thrower — From "The Star Thrower," an essay by Loren Eiseley in *The Star Thrower*, pp. 168-185, Harvest Books, 1978.

43 / How Dare You Love Yourself? — From *Only the Heart Knows How to Find Them* by Christopher DeVinck, Viking Penguin, 1993.

44 / Can It Be Beautiful Because It's Broken? — From *The Secret Garden* by Frances Hodgson Burnett, The Oxford Press, 1987.

48 / Where the Crowd Leads You — From *Don't Jump to Conclusions Without a Bungee Cord and Other Wise Advice: Devotions for Teens from the Book of Proverbs* by Martha Bolton, Servant Publications, 1999.

Contents

Contents Continued

Preface

Father Daniel Homan and I wrote the first volume of *Here I Am, Lord* because we wanted to serve two audiences: first, we hoped that teenagers would enjoy the book and use it to grow in prayer. But we also hoped that adults who love and serve youth would find it useful in their relationships and ministries. We realized that younger and older readers would use this book in different ways. We were right about that. We've both talked to teenagers and adults who have used the book and have found it helpful. If a book helps, in any small way . . . well, that's the most we can ask of a book.

What's different in this book? If you've used the first book you'll know the format and this is going to feel like an old friend. It consists of all new stories and new sessions (or chapters). But the format hasn't changed. Since the first volume was so well received we didn't want to change much, but rather to provide you with new material for more prayer and reflection.

First, however, who are "we"?

Both of us have worked with teenagers for many years. Father Homan as a Benedictine monk (and with his long-time partner in ministry Mary Cummings) has been surrounded by youth in the monastery's retreat house that has about four thousand teens pass through it yearly. Lonni is a parent to young adults and has taught teenagers how to write. She's also led youth groups, retreats, and seminars for many years since she was a teenager herself (which was a very long time ago). We've dedicated most of our lives to loving and serving teenagers. We have worked together and we have worked with others. This book flows from our work with so many gifted and wonderful teenagers.

The book also flows out of the Benedictine way of life. St. Benedict gave us a practical, realistic way to cope with the demands of real life. He teaches us to shape the ordinary into the way to God. We learn how to handle our lives. We learn about loving and community, about reverently touching and using, about imposing some sort of order and rhythm to our lives, about the high and holy value of work and leisure. The Rule of St. Benedict contains immense wisdom that makes enormous sense in our crowded lives. It is a way long practiced by Benedictine monks and nuns, but one that speaks squarely to contemporary people.

For the purpose of this book we have leaned heavily on the Benedictine practice *Lectio Divina*, a slow, prayerful way to read Scripture, as a means of exploring the text. You'll notice this in the way we use various stories and other material to make a single point and to direct the mind toward a single reflective topic.

We are indebted to the monastic community of St. Benedict Monastery in Oxford, Michigan, and the Sunday community of friends from whom we draw inspiration and support.

Our gratitude goes out to all those who love us and support us. A special thanks to Greg Erlandson at Our Sunday Visitor for his patience and belief in this project. We are especially indebted to the young people we have known and loved. They have taught us from the stories of their lives.

About This Book: A Note to Teens

A cynic once said: "Christians tell me that Jesus is the answer, but I want to know: What's the question?"

A clever remark. But maybe the cynic had forgotten what it was like to be young, and to have a million questions. Father Dan Homan and I have gotten to know many young people, and every one of them has had questions. Big questions. Why am I here? Who will love me? What's important and what's not? Why has this terrible thing happened to me? How shall I live my life?

We suspect that you ask questions like these too. Father Homan and I put this book together to help you wrestle with them. As you do, we think you will find answers too. Rather — an answer. The answer is not a philosophical concept, or a set of rules, or a blinding flash of mystical insight. The answer is a person — Jesus Christ. He lived in history and he's alive today. He is God's answer to human questions. The key to life, we believe, is getting into a relationship with Jesus. That's what we hope this book will help you do.

Too simple, you say? Glib? An easy religious formula for problems that hurt, that keep you awake at night?

We'll plead guilty to the charge of simplicity. Jesus is God's Word, and anyone can hear him. Men, women, and children who cannot read or write know him and love him. So do people whose minds do not work well, who suffer from the most terrible afflictions, who are starving, imprisoned, friendless, despised. They understand because Jesus is love, and every human being has a divine capacity to give and receive love. In the end, and in the beginning as well, the answer is simple.

But the fact that the answer is simple doesn't mean that it's easy. "It's not easy being green," sang Kermit the Frog. "It's not easy being a Christian," we sing back. It stands to reason that this would be so. Jesus was a human being, and it's not easy being a human being, as you well know. That means that God himself knows all your troubles and questions from the inside. He knows about failure and pain. He knows what it means to be lonely and misunderstood and rejected. He also knows the deep satisfactions of friendship, of love, of beauty and joy. Jesus is your all-knowing and all-loving companion on your journey. He is the best companion you could possibly have.

So get to know Jesus better. You get to know Jesus in the same way that you get to know any person by spending time with him, listening to him, talking to him. That's what this book is for. Think of it as a guidebook to communicating with your traveling companion — a sort of interactive telephone-computer-television-keyboard-reference book-journal that works only when you're alone at a time of relative peace and quiet. Father Homan and I have designed it to give you several different ways to get in touch with Jesus, your best and wisest friend. Here's how we've set it up.

Each of the sessions starts with **Something to Think About**. This is usually a story (you'll find a couple of poems and songs in there too) that illustrates the kind of hard-to-take problem that you run into all the time. Some of these are first-person stories from our own lives. Some are stories others have told us. Some are taken from books we've read.

Think about this story. We mean it. Take some time to reflect on it. Read it twice or three times if you want. What does the story mean to you? What issue is it presenting?

The next section is called **Making It Mine**. This is a reflection or commentary or even another story that looks at the theme from another point of view. It's an invitation for you to put yourself into the scene. The first section asks you to *think*. This section asks you to exercise your *imagination*. Ask, "What if this were me. . . ?"

Then you're invited to *pray*. The first part of the **Prayer Starter** section is a verse or two from Scripture. Most of these are quotes from the Psalms. The word "psalm" means "song." These are the ancient prayers of the Jewish people that Catholics and other Christians still pray every day. The Psalms are prayers in themselves; they are also excellent prayer "starters" — ways to begin to talk to God in a personal and sustained way.

The second part of the **Prayer Starter** section is a prayer that Father Homan and I have written. A couple are prayers associated with great Christians. These prayers are based on the theme of the day. We make no special claims for the eloquence and beauty of these prayers. They are intended to help *you* pray *your* prayer. As you pray, talk to Jesus. Talk to him about your feelings and thoughts. If you are burdened or sad or frightened or disappointed, admit your feelings to him. If you are excited or thrilled or bursting with enthusiasm, share these emotions with Jesus as well. Then listen to him. He will speak. Count on it. Jesus is love, and you can rest in his love.

The last section is called **Soul Writing**. We've given you room to do it right here in this book. We offer a suggestion for something for you to write about. Take up your pen and write. Express your feelings. Write down what the Lord said to you. Record any new insights you've had.

Writing comes easily for some people, hard for others. We encourage you to try it and stick with it even if it is difficult. Record what is happening to you. If you run short of time, jot down a few quick responses, perhaps key phrases that will jar your memory so you can write more when you have time later in the day. Just be sure to come back to it when you have more time. Write until you have nothing more to say.

Work out your pattern for going through this prayer journal. There are fifty sessions. You can do them in fifty consecutive days, five days a week for ten weeks, once a week for fifty weeks or other combinations. Some of you will be praying this book on your own. Others will be praying it with their youth group, on retreat, or with friends. If you are working through this book on your own, try to talk to someone else regularly about the issues that come up. You will find the journey is wonderfully richer when shared with a few trusted others.

Work on these prayer sessions at a time when you can be quiet inside. Some people can quiet their spirits in the middle of chaos, but most of us need a quiet place. Turn off the music. Go some place where you can be alone. Sit in a comfortable position with your back supported or lie on the floor. Take a few deep breaths, releasing each one slowly, and as each breath flows out of you, release tension and your hectic thinking patterns. You can learn to do this in just three or four minutes if you practice. Think of your body as being very heavy, as if made out of lead. Breathe deeply a few more times and when you feel quiet inside — begin reading.

You might start with the simple four-word prayer that is the title of this prayer journal: *Here I Am, Lord*. That's the main thing. The Lord is there for you too.

About This Book: A Note to Parents, Pastors, Teachers, and Youth Ministers

Here I Am, Lord is a book for prayer. Specifically, it's aimed at helping teenagers pray. It rests on a foundation of profound respect for the spiritual lives of young people and a conviction that God is already at work in their hearts. Some doubt this. They see teenagers lost in a fog of sex, drugs, rock 'n' roll, irony, aimlessness, and materialism. But we think that an excessive emphasis on these ills, as real as they are, is itself a kind of fog. Teens, by and large, wrestle with the same issues that adults do. They flee from the pressures of their lives in basically the same ways that adults do. And they are too often misunderstood, as too often adults are as well.

One thing we've learned is that teens pray. They don't talk about it to most adults, but they admit it among themselves. They hardly let a day get by without praying. They pray about personal concerns; they pray for their families and friends and for the world. They ask God hard questions. They shudder and cry and rage for only God to see. They reflect on decisions they are making and the things they are feeling. Teenagers are fierce about praying. Their prayer is strong, gritty, practical, and idealistic. That's the kind of prayer we hope to offer in these pages.

There are many ways this book can be used. Teens can pray the book on their own, over a period of time on a daily or weekly basis. A group of young people can use this book to pray together. It could be the core of a parish youth program or a Catholic school religion class. It can be read cover to cover or just opened to a page when the moment strikes. It is intended to launch prayer, to jump-start the experience. But it doesn't channel prayer in a particular way — except to point toward the Father, Son, and Holy Spirit. The young people praying will pray in their own ways, and their experiences of prayer will be different.

The format of the book is straightforward. There are fifty prayer sessions; each contains four parts. **Something to Think About** offers a reading to ponder — usually a story. **Making It Mine** suggests a personal application, sometimes by presenting another story, sometimes a personal reflection. The **Prayer Starter** offers two ways into personal prayer: some Scripture, usually some verses from the Psalms, and a prayer focused on the theme of the session.

The final section of each prayer sitting is called **Soul Writing**. This section introduces questions and thoughts that are intended to move the user from reflection to action. The system used is a modified kind of *Lectio Divina*, a Benedictine tradition of reflective, prayerful reading in which we open ourselves to hearing and being present to God.

Teachers, education directors, and youth ministers will find this book jammed with stories, illustrations, and lessons that can be used in many ways in work with young people.

An entire group who work through the prayer starters and stories together will find that community is built as they talk about the big issues and share themselves with the others in the group.

Facilitators can use these stories and reflection to launch discussion and keep it lively. They can use the material for youth meetings, retreats, special events — whenever they need to prepare a lesson or talk. Fifty stories should be about right for Lent or Advent and could be incorporated into any programs designed for these times of the year also.

In order to make the book easy to use, the chapter/sessions are numbered and often include simple introductions that set the stage. Each section is short; it could be read through in about five minutes.

If you like the authors and musicians you meet in these pages, you might want to follow up by finding more of their work in book and music stores. We quote writers and musicians whose work is popular with young people. Stories and music "work" — at least in our experience with the fairly large sample of American Catholic and other Christian teenagers who've come to our retreats and workshops and summer programs.

Prayer is not as much about the words we say to God as it is about hearing God and answering God. Prayer is about a relationship, and about living side by side with God, who is closer than our own breath, the Creator who shares every moment of our lives. Prayer is the adventure of a lifetime. We hope this book will enhance that adventure for many.

1
All Your Strength

Something to Think About

One Saturday morning a little boy was playing in his sandbox. He had the usual collection of cars and trucks, his bright plastic pail, and a sturdy plastic shovel. He set about to create tunnels and castles and shape a world with his own young hands. But in the middle of creating roads and carving tunnels in the soft sand he discovered a rock in the sand pile, a really big rock. He dug around it, he tried prying it out and, finally, by using his feet he managed to push it to the edge of the sandbox.

At the edge of the sandbox was a wooden wall that kept the sand inside; it was only about a foot high, but to this small boy it might as well have been six feet high, because try as hard as he could, he could not get the rock over the edge of the sandbox.

It's not that he wasn't trying. He shoved, he pried, he pushed. Yet each time he thought he was close, the thing rolled back into the sand. Finally, when the rock had rolled back onto his fingers he erupted into tears, and his father — who had been watching from the garage doorway close by — walked over to his son.

He reached down and gathered the little guy into his arms and brushed him off and said, "You made a brave attempt, son, but why didn't you use all of your strength, all the strength that is available to you?"

"I did, Daddy," he cried, "I used all the strength I have and it didn't move. I did use all my strength, Daddy!"

His father smiled and set the boy's feet on the grass. "No, son, you didn't," he said tenderly. "You didn't use all the strength you have; you didn't ask me." The father reached over and took the large rock into his hands and lifted it from the sandbox.

Life is like this: you'll run into obstacles that you are unable to move, that are simply beyond your abilities. But there is nothing beyond the ability of God.

Making It Mine

Rocks in your plans, rocks in your dreams, obstacles that keep you from creating the life and the "you" that you are working toward? Ever feel like you don't have what it takes to get rid of whatever's getting in your way?

"God is our refuge and our strength, an ever-present help in trouble" (Psalm 46:1).

Life is like this: you'll run into obstacles that you are unable to move, that are simply beyond your abilities. But there is nothing beyond the ability of God. God is your Father. God cares about what is happening in your sandbox. Prayer is how we talk with God. We don't need to take on the big battles alone; we have more strength than we know because we depend on more than our own strength.

In the same way, as Christians praying for one another, we have a joint strength. Have you ever tried to push your car out of a ditch by yourself? Pretty tough going, isn't it? But with a few friends pushing with you, it glides out as if the wheels are greased. When we pray for one another we join our strength together, and remarkable things happen.

If you have to do it all alone your strength will fail you. You can count on that. But when you join your strength to God's power and to the strength of your family and friends, you'll be able to move even the largest rocks that block your path.

Prayer Starter

I lift up my eyes to the hills;
where does my help come from?
My help comes from the Lord,
the Maker of heaven and earth.

Psalm 121:1-2

Father, I do not need to lean only on my own strength. For the rocks and obstacles, the problems that don't solve easily and the big things that get in my way, remind me to lean on your strength.

Soul Writing

Have you ever felt that you didn't have the strength to do something, that you were worn out with just the effort? What did you do? Did you pray about it? How might the situation have been different if you prayed about it or how did prayer impact the situation?

2
One Person

Something to Think About

The elderly member of the hospital's housekeeping staff was known for showing visitors the basement of the institution. In that dingy reminder of the past she showed visitors what looked like small prison cells with rusty bars.

She pointed and said, "That's where they used to keep Annie."

Annie was brought here when she was a young woman because her family thought she was incorrigible, which means they couldn't control her. She'd bite and scream; she threw her food at people. The doctors and nurses couldn't even examine her without her scratching and hitting and throwing herself around.

This much you can count on: if you treat someone well, if you give that person a chance, if you make some small gesture, that person will be better for it. . . .

I was only a few years younger than Annie, and I used to think how much I'd hate being locked up like that. I wanted to help, her screams were so horrible, but what could I do? I didn't know what to do, so I just did something I'm good at and baked her some brownies. I put them near her cell telling her they were for her and if she wanted them she could have them.

After that I'd talk to her sometimes, once I even got her laughing. She started behaving a little nicer when I was around. One of the nurses noticed it and asked if I would help them with Annie. Whenever they wanted to examine her I would go in the cage, calm her down, and hold her hand. That's how they discovered she was almost blind. She was glad for the discovery and felt that her actions had made a little bit of difference. That's not the end of the maid's story though.

The hospital tried to work with Annie, but it was still pretty tough. Then the Perkins Institute for the Blind opened. Annie was taught how to take care of herself; she was encouraged to learn independence and she grew into a confident, strong woman. She studied hard and became a teacher. Years later, Annie returned to where she had been locked up and offered her assistance as a teacher.

They had just received a letter from a man who wanted help with his daughter. She was unruly, both blind and deaf, and she was more than he could deal with. He wondered if they knew anyone who could live with them and teach his daughter.

So Annie Sullivan became the teacher and lifelong companion of Helen Keller. When Helen received the Nobel Prize she was asked who had the greatest impact on her life. Predictably, she answered it was Annie Sullivan. Annie corrected her, "No, Helen, the person who has had the most difference and impacted both our lives was a maid at the Tewksbury Institute."

Making It Mine

We can't begin to understand how our smallest acts of kindness impact not only those closest to us but the whole world around us. This much you can count on: if you treat someone well, if you give that person a chance, if you make some small gesture, that person will be better for it, even if you don't see the results or don't see anything dramatic.

And for that day or maybe that week that person will be a little kinder to someone. Such individuals like that might give someone a second chance; they might think twice before hurting themselves; they might even try a little harder. Then, the people they have treated better will do the same and the possibilities are endless for what can happen. You will probably never hear the stories of how people are improved by your small consideration. You might think it's not important when you talk to someone no one else talks to, or you mow someone's lawn, or you bake bread for a stranger in town.

But these little gestures are among the most important and most world-changing things you'll ever do. God uses us, uses our attempts at goodness to bring about all sorts of miraculous things. You've probably heard the story of Jesus feeding thousands of people with only a handful of fish and loaves of bread. That food was some boy's lunch. The miracle happened because one kid took the small thing he had and gave it away (see John 6:9).

The fact that a kid contributed to the miracle isn't even mentioned by three of the four Gospel writers — only John mentions the boy. The writers of the New Testament lived in an era when children and women were overlooked. John's New Testament writings are concerned with learning to love. In this loving, the little things are important, and so we discover a secret. Jesus took what a kid offered him and he multiplied it and used it to take care of thousands of people. That's what happens when you give Jesus whatever it is you have to give — even if you just give away your lunch.

Prayer Starter

"For my thoughts are not your thoughts,
neither are your ways my ways," declares the Lord.
"As the heavens are higher than the earth,
so are my ways higher than your ways
and my thoughts than your thoughts."

Isaiah 55:8-9

Lord, it is hard to see how the little things I do can make any difference at all. I'm not sure why even a little thing is hard for me sometimes, but you know it is. Give me courage to be kind, and compassion that asks, "What can I do?"

Soul Writing

Do you know anyone who makes a difference? Write about what that person does. What would you like to do that would make a difference?

3
What Awesome Really Means

Something to Think About

In 1982, author Annie Dillard and her husband witness a total eclipse of the sun. They are sitting on blankets among a mob of people on a high hillside.

Awe is the experience of discovering something that shatters all the boundaries, explodes out of our careful expectations, and tackles our senses with a direct hit.

The second before the sun went out, we saw a wall of dark shadow come speeding at us. We no sooner saw it than it was upon us, like thunder. It roared up the valley. It slammed our hill and knocked us out. It was the monstrous swift shadow cone of the moon. I have since read that this wave of shadow moves 1,800 miles an hour. Language can give no sense of this sort of speed — 1,800 miles an hour. It was 195 miles wide. No end was in sight; you saw only the edge. It rolled at you across the land 1,800 miles an hour, hauling darkness like plague behind it. Seeing it, and knowing it was coming straight for you, was like feeling a slug of anesthetic shoot up your arm. If you think very fast, you may have time to think: Soon it will hit my brain. You can feel the deadness race up your arm; you can feel the appalling, inhuman speed of your own blood. We saw the wall of shadow coming, and screamed before it hit.

This was the universe about which we have read so much and never before felt: the universe as a clockwork of loose spheres flung at stupefying, unauthorized speeds. How could anything moving so fast not crash, not veer from its orbit amok like a car out of control on a turn?

Less than two minutes later, when the sun emerged, the trailing edge of the shadow cone sped away. It coursed down our hill and raced eastward over the plain, faster than the eye could believe; it swept over the plain and dropped over the planet's rim in a twinkling. It had clobbered us, and now it roared away. We blinked into the light. . . . When the sun appeared as a blinding bead on the ring's side, the eclipse was over . . . the real world began there. I remember now: we all hurried away. . . . We never looked back. It was a general vamoose . . . enough is enough. One turns at least even from glory itself with a sigh of relief. From the depths of mystery, and even from the heights of splendor, we bounce back and hurry for the latitudes of home.

From *The Annie Dillard Reader* by Annie Dillard

 # Making It Mine

Awesome is a word of magnificence that has been trivialized to the point that nail polish and sunglasses can be "awesome." Author Annie Dillard describes an event in which actual awe happened. Most of us have only a few such experiences in a lifetime. She and her husband went to the side of the hill, with thousands of other people, to witness a total eclipse of the sun. She expected it to be interesting, even exciting. She got more than she expected.

Hillsides and mountaintops are common terrain for God. In Scripture we often hear of people talking to God and listening to God on mountains. Moses stumbled across a burning bush on a mountain and Jesus declared what we commonly call the Beatitudes on a high place. If you ever hike in the mountains or climb mountains or make it to the top of a mountain, you discover that awe is a tangible emotion. Of course, all of this makes it a good place for God to hang out.

It's difficult for us contemporary people to wrap our minds around something as huge as awe. We've learned to mistrust any experience that can't be calculated, analyzed, and categorized. Awe is the experience of discovering something that shatters all the boundaries, explodes out of our careful expectations, and tackles our senses with a direct hit.

Where there is genuine awe, you'll always find God lurking in the vicinity. Awe is so glorious it will scare the hell out of us, literally. Awe happens when somehow, in some split second, we get a glimpse of God, we get a sense that we are not alone in this big universe, and we realize that there is something out there, Someone who is much bigger than we are. It is the crackling-with-magic moment when we first realize that while we are a great many splendid things, we are not God.

Awe rushes into us and slams us against a wall of divinity and blinds us with glory, and leaves us to return to our ordinary lives with a firm knowledge that behind all this ordinary stuff there is something more substantial and dazzling then we understand.

Next time someone says a new motorcycle is awesome, tell that person it just ain't so.

Prayer Starter

My heart is not proud, O Lord,
my eyes are not haughty;
I do not concern myself with great matters
or things too wonderful for me.
But I have stilled and quieted my soul;
like a weaned child with its mother,
like a weaned child is my soul within me.

Psalm 131:1-2

Awesome God, a life without wonder would be the most boring kind of life. Open my eyes to the magnificence of your creation and the marvels of being alive and being in your presence. Give me a heart that is open to awe and the wisdom and genuine encounters with the real thing.

Soul Writing

Write about an experience or something that happened which caused you to experience genuine awe. What did it feel like? Write a prayer describing it to God.

4
What Kind of Power Does God Have?

Something to Think About

Author Philip Yancey describes his trip to Russia "when the Soviet Empire was crumbling."

Mikhail Gorbachev was giving way to Boris Yeltsin, and the entire nation was trying to rediscover itself. The iron grasp of power had loosened, and people were now reveling in the freedom to say whatever they wished.

I remember vividly a meeting with the editors of *Pravda*, formerly the official mouthpiece of the Communist Party. *Pravda* as much as any institution had slavishly served the Communist "church." Now, though, *Pravda*'s circulation was falling dramatically (from eleven million to seven hundred thousand) in concert with communism's fall from grace. The editors seemed shaken to the core. So shaken that they were now asking advice from emissaries of a religion their founder had scorned as the "opiate of the people."

The editors remarked wistfully that Christianity and communism have many of the same ideals: equality, sharing, justice, and racial harmony. Yet they had to admit the Marxist pursuit of that vision had produced the worst nightmares the world has ever seen. Why?

"We don't know how to motivate the people to show compassion," said the editor in chief. "We tried raising money for the children of Chernobyl, but the average Russian would rather spend his money on drink. How do you reform and motivate people? How do you get them to be good?"

Seventy-four years of communism had proved beyond all doubt that goodness could not be legislated from the Kremlin and enforced at the point of a gun. In a heavy irony, attempts to compel morality tend to produce defiant subjects and tyrannical rulers who lose their moral core. Goodness cannot be imposed externally, from the top down; it must grow internally, from the bottom up. With a bullwhip or a billy club

Goodness cannot be imposed externally, from the top down; it must grow internally, from the bottom up.

or an AK-47, human beings can force other human beings to do just about anything they want.

God's power, in contrast, is internal and noncoercive. In its commitment to transform gently from the inside out and in its relentless dependence on human choice, God's power may resemble a kind of abdication.

"God is not a Nazi," said Thomas Merton. Indeed God is not.

From *The Jesus I Never Knew* by Philip Yancey

Making It Mine

We hear the text every Holy Thursday: Jesus takes up the basin and towel and stoops down to wash the feet of baffled, offended, grumbling men — one of whom would soon take those feet to a place of betrayal.

One July day, a retreat I had worked with two close friends, Jon and Philip, came to an end. The three of us had been cooks and kitchen help. It meant three days on our feet, on concrete floors. This particular church wasn't well equipped. Every task seemed to mean bending and stretching and reaching. Even my toenails ached.

It was Sunday evening. It was over. And Lake Huron was only steps away from our door. Cold, refreshing Lake Huron. The three of us flopped into my car and dashed for the water.

We removed sneakers and socks, rolled up our shorts and sleeves, then ran into the water. We stayed there at least half an hour, splashing, laughing, talking about the weekend, the food, the fun.

As the sun started setting, the three of us headed up the beach to my car, covering our legs up to the knees with a wet coat of sand.

We got to my car. Jon opened a rear door, looked at the spotless interior, glanced down at his legs, reached inside for a towel. Phil looked at Jon as if to say, "What do we do?" Jon said, "Sit down and give me your feet."

Jon stooped over and began wiping sand from Phil's feet. The picture struck me. The man with the towel was African-American, and the man whose feet were surrendered for wiping was Caucasian. Moments later, Jon motioned for me to sit on the edge of the car. He wiped the sand from my legs and feet also. As soon as he finished, Phil took the towel from him. Kneeling, he wiped the sand from Jon's feet and ankles.

I kept the towel in the trunk of my car for the rest of summer and most of fall. Just seeing it occasionally transported me back to the beach where I had watched a parable come to life.

Love, goodness, service — these values can't be forced at the point of a gun or coerced by rules. We do need to abdicate our self-centered quest for power. We do need to grow in love and goodness. Our "abdication" though is not to One who holds a gun, but a towel.

 # Prayer Starter

You guide the humble in doing right
and teach your way to the lowly.
All your paths, O Lord, are love and faithfulness
to those who keep your covenant and your testimonies.

Psalm 25:8-9

Faithful God, surrendering to you is very hard. Sometimes I'd rather fight for something I don't really want than take what you give that I need. Give me a humble heart. Show me how to love you, not fear you.

Soul Writing

Write about your ideas of who God is. Which is easier to believe — that God loves you and serves you or that God is waiting (somewhat eagerly) to punish you when you mess up?

5
No Struggle, No Flight

Something to Think About

A man found an emperor moth's cocoon and took it home because he wanted to observe the moth emerging from it. He watched the cocoon faithfully, and one day he noticed a slight opening in it. For several hours the moth struggled to get out of the cocoon. It looked like the moth wasn't making much progress; in fact, as far as the man could tell, the little moth was wedged into the cocoon, stuck and unable to move any more.

Out of concern the man decided to help the moth get out. He used scissors to carefully snip off the cocoon. Soon the moth emerged. Its body was swollen and its wings were shriveled and tiny. The man continued to watch, expecting the swelling to go down and the wings to stretch and expand. He watched, and nothing happened. The insect spent the rest of its life with a swollen body and shriveled wings, unable to do what it had been created to do — fly.

The cocoon is designed to restrict and compress on the moth, forcing fluid from its body into the wings and making it able to fly. It is a difficult process, but God designed it that way. Yes, it was a struggle to get free, but the moth can't fly without the struggle. The man with his best intentions had crippled the moth by trying to make it too easy for the insect.

Sometimes we wish that God would go easy on us; we wish parents would go easier; we wish our friends could understood us better. . . . No one would be doing you a favor if they let up too much though.

Making It Mine

Sometimes we wish that God would go easy on us; we wish parents would go easier; we wish our friends could understood us better and that teachers were a little less demanding. No one would be doing you a favor if they let up too much though.

You may wonder at times why God doesn't come to your rescue. After all, you do your best and you're a good person. Yet you wrestle with yourself, your failures, the messes you make, the obstacles to your dreams, and you feel like you're doing it alone sometimes.

You aren't alone. God doesn't rescue us all the time because sometimes the struggle is what makes us strong. In overcoming obstacles, we discover what we're made of. No, it isn't easy. Most of the time you're going to wish for a different way. But you do want to fly, don't you?

Prayer Starter

Stand at the crossroads and look;
ask for the ancient paths,
ask where the good way is, and walk in it,
and you will find rest for your souls.

Jeremiah 6:16

God of my dreams, yes, I do want to fly. But I'm bone-weary sometimes and don't know how I'm going to go on. Give me wind under my wings, and strength to keep trying.

Soul Writing

What is happening right now that you would like God to rescue you from? Write about why you want to be rescued and then write about what will happen if you have to continue struggling.

6
Love Letters

Something to Think About

Mark Eklund liked to talk. Sister Helen, his third-grade teacher said he talked incessantly. He belonged to a class of twenty-three students who lived in a rural area and went to church together. Mark was well-liked and something of a class clown. His teacher remembers getting annoyed with him one day when he was talking far too much and she snapped at him, "If you say one more word, I am going to tape your mouth shut!" A few seconds later one of the other students blurted out, "Mark is talking again."

"I remember the scene as if it had occurred this morning," Sister Helen said. "I walked to my desk, very deliberately opened my drawer, and took out a roll of masking tape and made a big X over his mouth. . . . As I glanced at Mark to see how he was doing, he winked at me. That did it! I started laughing. The class cheered as I walked back to Mark's desk, removed the tape, and shrugged my shoulders. His first words were, 'Thanks for correcting me, Sister.' "

What a difference a few positive words would have made.

Before long the teacher had started teaching junior-high math and before she knew it Mark was in her class again. He was even more well-liked. She remembers him as a handsome boy with a big smile who was always polite. He didn't talk as much, mostly because they were learning "new math" and the ninth graders were having trouble with some of the concepts. Before long the students were barking at one another and their teacher, and a general attitude of "crankiness" took over the math room.

"I had to stop the negative talk before it got out of hand," the teacher said. "I asked them to list the names of each of their classmates and to think of the nicest thing they could say about each of their classmates and write it down. It took the remainder of the period. . . . Eventually, I collected the comments on one piece of paper and gave each student his or her list. Before long the entire class was smiling, 'Really?' I heard whispered. 'I never knew that meant anything to anyone.' 'I didn't know others liked me.' No one ever mentioned those papers in class. . . . That group of students moved on."

Several years later Sister Helen heard that Mark had been killed in Vietnam. His parents asked her to attend the funeral. "All I could think of at that moment was that I would give all the masking tape in the world if he could talk to me."

The church was jammed with Mark's friends. It rained that day. Mark's sister sang "The Battle Hymn of the Republic" and the bugler played taps. One by one, those who had known and loved Mark walked by the coffin and sprinkled it with holy water.

At the funeral luncheon, Mark's father took a wallet out of his pocket, telling Sister Helen that he had found it in his son's belongings, and he pulled out a carefully folded and taped piece of paper that had obviously been opened and refolded many times. "I knew without looking that the paper was the one on which I had listed all the good things his classmates had to say about him," Sister Helen said.

"Thank you for doing that," his mother said. "As you can see, he treasured it." Gathering around, many of Mark's classmates said they also still had their lists. "Mine is still in my top drawer," one said. "I married someone in your class and he asked me to put it in our wedding album," said another. Then a woman from the class reached into her purse, found her wallet, and removed her list. "I carry it with me all the time," she said.

 # Making It Mine

It's so easy to be critical. Most of us have a knack for finding fault and then pointing out that fault to everyone, especially the one with the fault. Even when it's only little comments, they chip away at a person's self-worth, one sliver at a time. It's probably happened to you.

Jerry was a busy man with a full life. He was a landscape designer who worked out of his home. His young brother Will lived with him, as did his wife and daughter. It was Will's tenth birthday. He waited all day for someone to wish him "happy birthday"; it didn't happen. On his way home from school the boy gave himself a pep talk. His brother was an important and busy man. He wasn't used to having Will around; they were all adjusting after their mother's long illness and death. His brother wasn't a selfish man, just a busy one.

Will decided to do something nice for his brother. He stopped at a roadside stand and picked up a small basket of peaches. Their mother had always made them peach pies. Running into the house Will burst into Jerry's office and put the basket on his desk, exclaiming, "Look, I got this for you!"

Jerry was on the phone. He covered the mouthpiece and said, "You're late again, Will. If you aren't going to come straight home from school I expect you to be courteous enough to tell us your plans. Go to your room." Will has never forgotten his tenth birthday. He says that day set in stone how he and Jerry would relate to one another. Will says, "To this day I feel like no matter what I do, my brother will find fault."

What a difference a few positive words would have made.

 # Prayer Starter

I said, "I will watch my ways
and keep my tongue from sin;
I will put a muzzle on my mouth. . . ."

Psalm 39:1a

Reckless words pierce like a sword,
but the tongue of the wise brings healing.

Proverbs 12:18

God, speech is a gift. Teach me to use it wisely, to guard my words. Every day help me make the choice to use my words for healing rather than destroying.

Soul Writing

Write a letter to a friend describing what you like most about him or her. Do the same for a member of your family. Write a letter to yourself about what you like about yourself.

7
What Do People Need?

Something to Think About

There is an old Irish ditty: "To live above with the saints we love, ah, that is the purest glory. But to live below with the saints we know, ah that's another story." In reflecting on how we see other people, I am reminded of a time in my life right after ordination. The oils of ordination were still wet upon my hands when I was asked to give a priests' retreat. Having a lot of mileage on my mouth already, I accepted.

However, when I got there and saw my retreatants filing into the chapel for the first conference, I was shocked by a sudden realization. I was going to be the youngest man in that chapel by at least fifteen years. And I was going to be preaching to these considerably older men for a whole week. There were two bishops also, which added to my considerable terror. I was standing there watching them enter the chapel with the monsignor who directed the retreat house. With a friendly smile, the monsignor asked, "How do you feel?"

I replied, "Scared!"

"Scared? Why?"

"Didn't you see them?"

The monsignor then came over to me, put a paternal arm around my shoulder, and said, "They just need what everybody else needs: a little love and understanding. And I remember asking him, 'Why don't they look like it?' " Is this what people really need — a little love and understanding? Of course they do, but you and I often wonder, "Why don't they look like it?"

Seasons of the Heart by John Powell,
originally from the video *Free to Be Me*

What do people need most? Love and understanding. It's true of all of us. It is most true of those who don't look like it. Some people are harder to love.

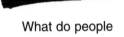

Making It Mine

What do people need most? Love and understanding. It's true of all of us. It is most true of those who don't look like it. Some people are harder to love. You know the kind I mean. You have an uncle like that or a friend's friend or a teacher or someone who rides your bus.

Lois was hard to love. She was two years older than me. She was also confined to a wheelchair and had a nasty disposition. I felt compassion for her, but I couldn't like her. When I was a young girl, short little white boots, called go-go boots, became very popular. I was in seventh grade when I got mine. I walked into the library wearing them and across the room I heard her screech, "Hey, Miss Go-Go Boots!"

I turned to look at her snarling face and, as young as I was, it became clear to me that the reason she was taunting me was really very simple: I was standing up in my go-go boots. I could dance in my go-go boots, and if I didn't like what she was saying, I could take my go-go boots and walk away. She had none of those options.

I don't know how long I stood there looking at her with a great ache filling me up, an ache with her name on it. It must have been a long time because she was looking pretty uneasy. In that instant I saw how desperately she needed to be understood. It was as if she was calling out, "Please ignore how rude and mean-tempered I am; please get past that and care about me."

I never did learn to like Lois. But I slowly learned to understand her better and when I understood her, she lost the power to intimidate me.

I've made a point of trying to understand people. It's a life skill that has served me well. I can't remember the last time anyone has intimidated me. People cease to be frightening when we understand them. The best thing about understanding people better is that I have also come to like them better.

 # Prayer Starter

The Lord is gracious and compassionate,
slow to anger and rich in love.
The Lord is good to all;
he has compassion on all he has made.

Psalm 145:8-9

God, all of your creation is wondrous, every rock and every person. We don't often understand the glorious and bizarre ways we are gifted and different. Give me insight to understand and a heart big enough to love the ones different from me.

Soul Writing

Write about someone you don't understand. Try to get into that person's skin and understand his or her behavior. If you were that person what would you want from others? Describe the kind of understanding you'd like to receive. How can you start giving that kind of understanding to others?

8
The Winds of God's Will

Something to Think About

The author's brother is a grandfather who is spending the day with his two grandchildren before the children move across the country with their father. His brother was always a "curmudgeon" and proud of it. But his two little grandchildren had transformed him into a different, more tender kind of man; and they were leaving. So, the author suggests to his brother that he grab the kids and go fly kites.

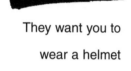

They want you to wear a helmet when you decide to leap out of the nest. It is a frightening time for parents and young adults. So be kind to one another.

I was left with the image of two little children excitedly holding on to a kite string, with no concern at all about their future. Their laughter still echoed inside me on the drive home as I reflected on just how much God's will is like flying a kite. Seemingly invisible forces determine whether or not a kite will become airborne. Those winds can grab hold of the kite so powerfully that they carry it to heights that are limited only by the length of the string.

But just as quickly, those same forces can drop the kite into an irreversible tailspin. All of this is done in what appears to be an arbitrary senseless pattern. No amount of scientific knowledge will help us know what God's will is for us. So we shouldn't always be asking about it and questioning it. Sometimes it is better just to go for the ride and trust those invisible winds.

Making It Mine

Trust couldn't have been easy for Mary. She had held the boy while he had a fever. She taught him to walk. She watched him hammer his first nail in Joseph's workshop. She knew about his first broken heart and she had listened to his questions about what God expected and wanted from him.

Tucked into some corner of her memory were the words of an angel, the truth about his birth, and the memory that this son of hers was not like any other human being ever born. But he had been born after all, born to her. She had protected him, held him, kept him close to her all these years.

And now, he was boarding up the carpenter shop. He was talking about a kingdom you couldn't see. He was calling fishermen to follow him. He was stirring up neighbors and friends and relatives, this beautiful strong boy of hers. He had changed her life. And she would be alone when he shut the door behind him.

How did she trust? She must have wondered if the winds of God would lift him up or crash him to the ground. She had to wonder if it was all just a big mistake. Maybe he'd marry a nice girl and give her grandchildren. Maybe he'd stay and work Joseph's business. Maybe . . .

No. He wasn't going to do that. He was going. And she would have to find it in herself to let him go. She would have to release him to the will of God. Nothing is more frightening than that for a mother or father. When your parents look at you, they have the same feeling. They want only the best for you. They want you to follow hard after whatever God's will is for you, but they'd like you to do it in the neighborhood and they want you to wear a helmet when you decide to leap out of the nest. It is a frightening time for parents and young adults. So be kind to one another.

 # Prayer Starter

Lord, you have assigned me my
portion and my cup;
you have made my lot secure.
The boundary lines have fallen for me in pleasant places;
surely I have a delightful inheritance.

Psalm 16:5-6

God, the mystery of your will draws me to places I've never been before and I suspect I am becoming someone I've never been. I go with my head high and my heart fixed on you. Reassure those who love me that I will be safe. Reassure me that I am going somewhere and this journey matters.

Soul Writing

What do you believe is God's will for you? How is your understanding of God's will changing? Imagine talking to someone you admire about what God's will means. Write out that conversation.

9
Can You Be Too Positive?

Something to Think About

Michael is the kind of guy you love to hate because he's always got something positive to say. If you asked him how he's doing he'd say something like, "If I were any better I would be twins!"

You'd think he is the son of a motivational speaker for sure.

Let someone have a bad day and Michael would point out the positive side. That can get annoying. If you had a problem he'd say something like, "Every problem has a solution — that's what problems are for."

People who live with difficult circumstances and choose to live with a positive attitude are the heroes. . . . They are a witness to the triumph of the human spirit.

His unrelenting positive attitude has made more than one person curious about him. If you ask him how he manages to be so positive he'll tell you something like this: "I get up and say to myself, 'Mike, you have a choice today. You can be in a good mood or you can be in a bad mood.' I choose to be in a good mood. When something bad happens I can decide to be a victim and let it beat me or I can learn from it. I can accept other's complaining or I can point to the positive. I'd rather look at the positive."

"Yeah, right," they all say to Michael. "You just decide to live in wonderland." Michael smiles. "It really is about choices. You choose how you'll react to any situation. Strip life down to the bone and you discover a set of choices. The bottom line is that you'll make your own life with your choices."

Sounds like a nice but impractical theory, doesn't it?

Michael was involved in an accident. He fell off a communications tower and plummeted sixty feet. After eighteen hours of surgery and weeks of intensive care, he was released from the hospital, his body still weak and broken, with rods in his back and legs.

I saw him six months after his accident. I said, "How you doing, Michael?"

He grinned and said, "If I were any better I'd be twins. Wanna see my scars?"

I declined on the scars but asked him what went through his mind during the accident and his recovery.

"First thing I thought of was my daughter who was about to be born," he said. "I lay on the ground and later in the hospital and told myself that I had a choice. I could choose to live or I could choose to die. I chose to live." He said the paramedics were great and kept saying he'd be fine. "But I could read it in their eyes, 'Man, he's dead.'" Someone asked me whether I was allergic to anything and I told them, "Yeah, gravity." They all laughed. Then I told them that I knew I was in bad shape, but they should treat me like a living man, not a dead man. I choose to live, then and now."

 ## Making It Mine

Recently one of the television magazines did a story about a woman who says she has chosen to die. She is a paraplegic, confined to a wheelchair, with others taking care of her. The camera zoomed in on her round face. She said no one had a right to keep her alive when she had chosen to die.

But she wasn't telling the truth. She has not chosen to die. How can I be so sure? She was wearing a bright red dress, her makeup was flawless, and she had richly glowing pearls on her ears and at her throat. Her dark hair was styled fashionably, her nails perfectly manicured. These are not the actions of a woman who has made a decision to die. Not only did she want to live, she wanted others to notice her living. A person who has given up doesn't have her shining dark hair styled or her slim fingernails manicured. When she opens her eyes and wants to brush her teeth she is making a choice to live another day. She doesn't have to do it. She makes the choice whether she admits it or not.

People all around you, people who live with difficult circumstances, choose to live with a positive attitude. These are the heroes, the courageous ones among us. They are a witness to the triumph of the human spirit.

Prayer Starter

My flesh and my heart may fail,
but God is the strength of my heart
and my portion forever.

Psalm 73:26

This day I call heaven and earth as a witness. . . . I have set before you life and death. . . . Now choose life, so that you and your children may live and that you may love the Lord your God, listen to his voice, and hold fast to him.

Deuteronomy 30:19-20a

Lord, my life is good. I don't always remember that, but I know it's true. I could be more positive sometimes. Teach me to make good life-giving decisions for myself and all the people who care about me.

Soul Writing

Think about the ways you make a decision every day to choose life. What do you think God is asking of the people when he tells them to choose life in the biblical passage from Deuteronomy?

What makes life worthwhile for you? How would a more positive attitude make a difference for you?

10
Shivering Magic

Something to Think About

Actual belief in miracles was mixed among us boys, although all of us watched the priests' hands with awe at the instant the Host was changed into the living, breathing Body of Christ. We did not expect to actually see the change steal over the Host itself, as we had been told ad infinitum by the nuns that the miracle was beyond human ken; but we did half expect to see a priest's hands burst spontaneously into flame as he handled the distilled essence of the Mind that invented the universe. There was some discussion about what we should do if a hand fire broke out. There were two general camps: the first insisted that the water cruet should be flung at the fire, and the second advised a sprint away from the awful miracle and toward the janitor. . . .

Before you reject or embrace anything, be sure you know what it is you're responding to. Find the ultimate truths and hold on to these.

I could never turn my eyes away from that key moment, though. It was and is the single most mysterious and bizarre belief of my faith, and it was in many ways the thing that set us apart from all other Christian denominations. In later years I would sit in Congregationalist and Episcopalian and Lutheran services and observe the communions of those faiths . . . and while these acts seemed friendlier to me, more communal than the shivering magic of the Transubstantiation, they seemed insubstantial too, muted, more like a casual brunch than a heartbreaking Last Supper.

I always wanted to like the communions of other faiths, but they seemed pale to me. I suppose being dipped in miracles every day inoculates you against the mundane.

From *Credo* by Brian Doyle

Making It Mine

Once there was a small village where an old man who made and repaired clocks lived. Whenever any clock in the village went a bit wacky he could fix it, and the watches too. Everyone in the village depended on this sole, aging clockmaker to keep their timepieces in working order.

The inevitable happened. He died, leaving no children, no apprentice. No one in the village could fix clocks. After a little while, as had always happened, various village clocks and watches began to break down. A clock would strike midnight at two in the afternoon or announce high noon at ten in the morning. Eventually the clocks became unreliable, more annoyance than value, and the villagers abandoned their timepieces.

One day, several years later, a famous clockmaker and repairer passed through the village. The people crowded around him, pushing and begging for him to fix their dead and broken clocks and watches. He was a kind man and spent long hours and several days looking at all the timepieces.

Finally, he announced that he could repair some of the timepieces, but only some. He could repair the ones that had been kept wound by their owners. These timepieces, though weak and broken, would be able to "remember" how to keep time.

Tradition is like these timepieces: it is a way for us to remember how to keep time, how to align our lives, how to know what matters most. One way to think about tradition would be to consider it a method by which something that is too important to forget is underlined.

Growing up involves determining for yourself if you believe something is true. It means you will look at the Catholicism of your family and friends, the tradition that has been instilled in you, and you will decide whether or not you want a life "dipped in miracles." In the process of growing, thinking, praying, and deciding, it's important that you keep the watch (your faith) wound, even if you doubt you'll ever use it again. Life is going to surprise you and you might find yourself glad you kept it in working order.

Go to Mass. Really hear what is going on. Pray even when the sky seems made of tin. Before you reject or embrace anything, be sure you know what it is you're responding to. Find the ultimate truths and hold on to these. Keep your spirit wound, even when it doesn't make much sense to you. Our relationships, our dreams, faith, prayers — these must be wound day after day, practiced when it seems meaningless. We go through the motions sometimes just so we don't forget the motions. Love when your heart is broken, believe when faith seems pointless, get out of bed when pain is the only reality — that's how you keep the watch of faith wound.

Brian Doyle is right. Ours is a tradition in which we are dipped in the miraculous. We are in over our heads in the splintering, breathtaking wonder of God among us. We hold these things to be more than images or ideas or symbols. We know that when we participate in the Eucharist we are taking God into ourselves. We are inhaling the substance of the Divine. God becomes part of us and we are part of him. It takes a faith bigger than anything you've ever seen. A faith that might take you more than fifteen or twenty or thirty years to grow into. Though it takes a lifetime, don't give up. Keep showing up. Keep winding the watch.

 # Prayer Starter

Can a mother forget the baby at her breast
and have no compassion on the child she has borne?
Though she may forget,
I will not forget you!
See, I have engraved you on the palms of my hands; . . .

Isaiah 49:15-16a

God, can I admit my doubts to you? I want to believe. My faith isn't very big right now, but I offer it to you with the best of my intentions to believe. Help me stay open to every miraculous moment. Help me believe.

Soul Writing

Do you have doubts about faith and Christianity? Write about your faith and your doubts. Copy it on a separate sheet from this book and fold it up into a small square. Take the folded paper out to a woods or in your backyard and plant it in the ground with these words: "God, here is the truth about what I think and feel. Make it grow into whatever you know it should be. I will keep trying to trust you."

11
The Way Home

Something to Think About

In her book Traveling Mercies, *author Anne LaMott tells about a woman who came to her church to minister to the parish.*

"You wanna go to Mass with my family on Sunday?" He grinned. Sean had discovered he could always find his way home from that holy place.

She sings to us sometimes from the pulpit and she tells us stories of when she was a child. She told us this story just the other day: When she was about seven, her best friend got lost one day. The little girl ran up and down the streets of the big town where they lived, but she couldn't find a single landmark. She was very frightened. Finally a policeman stopped to help her. He put her in the passenger seat of his car, and they drove around until she finally saw her church. She pointed it out to the policeman, and the she told him firmly, "You could let me out now. This is my church, and I can always find my home from here."

And that is why I have stayed so close to mine; because no matter how bad I am feeling, how lost or lonely or frightened, when I see the faces of the people at my church, and hear their tawny voices, I can always find my way home.

From *Traveling Mercies* by Anne LaMott

Making It Mine

I've never gone so far that I've forgotten my way home.
The best things always bring us round again.
Over and over.

From "Don't Let the Dust Get in Your Eyes,"
an unpublished song by Russ Taft

Sean was sixteen when he became an uncle for the first time. We were biology partners and almost daily he showed me pictures of his little niece. She was a doll with lots of curls and dimples and chubby little hands and knees. Her name was Heather.

When Sean didn't show up at school for a few days I heard

from a friend of his that Heather had died. SIDS — Sudden Infant Death Syndrome. She was fine one day and gone the next. Sean and his whole family were shattered. I wrote Sean a note and sent him a small baby bracelet with the words "Heather's Uncle" made up of tiny pink, green, and white beads. He called me a few days later and asked if I'd have a soda with him

He fought tears as he said it wasn't fair that Heather would never see a snowflake or watch cartoons or dance on her toes or play baseball or learn to color. He said God wasn't fair and that's why he had stopped going to church. This only proved what he already knew. I was barely sixteen years old myself and didn't feel qualified to speak for God. He talked for an hour or two and then we left. We headed for my house about four blocks away. We walked in silence and as we rounded the corner it occurred to me that we were going to walk right past the church where Sean had been baptized.

Sean's steps slowed as we walked by the church. He paused, then went inside. Sean went to the front of the church. He stood there clenching his fists and choking with bottled-up rage. Then he started sobbing, great big adult man-sized tears. It suddenly felt all wrong watching him, so I slipped out and walked home alone.

Sean returned to school a few days later. He sat beside me at our table talking as if nothing had happened. About fifty-five minutes later the bell rang and we gathered our things. Once we got out in the hallway he reached for my book bag and asked, "You wanna go to Mass with my family on Sunday?" He grinned. Sean had discovered he could always find his way home from that holy place.

Prayer Starter

If anyone loves me, he will obey my teaching. My Father will love him, and we will come to him and make our home with him.

John 14:23

Father, I get lost sometimes. I don't know how to make sense of everything and I don't know how to get myself to a safe place. I'm trusting you to get me home when I don't know how to get there.

Soul Writing

What does church mean to you? Why does church have the meaning for you that it does? In what way can a community of faith turn you toward home when you've gotten off track?

12
Questionable Evidence

Something to Think About

The author visits his friend and mother-in-law, Ruby, who lives on a farm in southern Indiana. Ruby knows all the stories of all the people and all the apple orchards around her.

One day I was visiting, and Ruby called me to the window.

"Listen to that," she said. I listened and heard a bird give five short "who's."

"What is it?" I asked.

"A rain crow," she said. "You hear them before a big rain. I've never seen one, but I've heard them plenty of times."

That was a new one on me, but I wasn't about to argue with Ruby. . . . It rained two hours later.

The Gospel of John tells us about the resurrected Jesus visiting the disciples, and Thomas not believing it was Jesus until he touched the wounds. John tells us how Jesus said, "Blessed are those who have not seen and yet believe" (John 20:29). A lot of smart people say John wrote at a time when the folks who had known Jesus were dead and gone. So John told his story to reassure early Christians that you can believe in something you've never seen. Kind of like Ruby believing in the rain crows.

We're all Missourians at heart, inclined toward the "Show me!" mentality. Except every now and then we bump into Jesus and rain crows, where seeing doesn't come easy. . . . Sometimes the most real things are the things we cannot see.

From *Front Porch Tales* by Philip Gulley

God, like love, must be experienced.

Making It Mine

Have you ever heard someone who believes in God trying to offer proof for God's existence? These are the usual arguments:

1. Since the beginning of history as we know it, people have believed in gods or God.

2. The universe is so complex that there must be an intelligent originator of it.

3. Even in the most primitive of cultures we discover an inherent need, as if built into the DNA, for truth, goodness, justice, beauty, love, and, under one form or another, God.

4. Every age has produced mystics and saints who experience something beyond the normal scope of reality and speak of this Other in sacred divine terms.

These are compelling statements, but it doesn't take much thought to discover that none of these arguments are watertight. And none of them, even the full weight taken together, is going to convince anyone of God's existence unless that person is predisposed to believe anyway. The truth is that it is impossible to prove or disprove that God is real. Humanity is not equipped to prove God exists. We drive people away with our arguments and evidences.

Like it or not, if we believe in God, we have to accept that this is how God arranged it. God apparently does not require our meagerly attempts at defending him. I'm certain God appreciates our efforts, but it is much like trying to prove that love exists. Unless one has been loved, unless one has loved, there is no convincing anyone of the reality.

God moves in the sphere of faith. We experience God in no other way. One theologian has likened it to "a leap-into-the-darkness-of-mystery leap of faith." Do not hesitate to believe and believe deeply. However, those around you are not likely to believe that you believe unless, somehow, they experience what you believe by your actions and choices. God, like love, must be experienced.

 # Prayer Starter

Faith is being sure of what we hope for and certain of what we do not see. . . . By faith we understand that the universe was formed at God's command, so that what is seen was not made out of what was visible.

Hebrews 11:1, 3

Faithful Father, my faith is not as big as I think it should be, but I do have faith. For all the moments when I doubt, remind me that even doubt will help me grow in faith. Don't let me fear my questions; instead, teach me to open my heart to you so that I might have more faith and believe more deeply.

Soul Writing

What questions would you like to ask God? What strengthens your faith? What feeds your doubt? What kinds of things are you doing to build faith (examples: attend Mass, read spiritual books, pray, etc.)? What are the opposite things you do that might tear down your faith? What steps will you take to increasingly encourage your own faith?

13
Tell It Like It Is

Something to Think About

Most of you have probably heard the story "The Emperor's New Clothes." It's more of a parable than it is a story. The story (slightly updated) goes that in a faraway place there lived a powerful emperor who was quite impressed with himself. That's probably the usual state of people like emperors and dictators, so that's no surprise.

The emperor believed that money could buy the finest of things and when it came time for him to purchase a new set of clothing he commissioned the finest designer in the world. The designer came highly recommended by others and his work was obviously very impressive to these people.

When he announced a few weeks later that the emperor's new clothes were ready . . . well, to say the least, the emperor was excited. Naturally he wanted to share the moment with other people, his family, for example, and all the people who worked in the palace; so he had everyone gather in the throne room and announced the royal designer, who came in holding magnificent golden hangers.

"And you will notice the red satin on the cuffs. . . . Ah, yes, and these buttons are made of pearls from the coldest waters overlaid with gold that was polished by seventeen youths. . . . The fabric was spun by none other than a princess using yarns from her private collection interwoven with real silver. . . ."

"My, my, my . . ." the emperor murmured as he sat up very straight and nodded his head and oohed and aahed as seemed appropriate. So did the rest of the people in the room. However, nearly everyone in the room was wondering if anyone else noticed . . . well, no . . . of course not, it must be their own eyes . . . but weren't those hangers empty?

However, they decided that the clothing must be so fine that one had to have royal eyes to see the magnificent clothing. In fact, one of the subjects suggested that they have a parade so that the emperor could show everyone his fine new attire. The emperor thought it was a marvelous idea! And so that's what they did.

Telling the truth, that's the strength of youth. Unless we teach them otherwise, the young will say what they think, what they really think.

Out of the palace rode the emperor, having changed into the new royal robes, sitting high on the shoulders of twelve men, on his royal throne carried on golden poles. A hundred trumpeters went before him, with callers announcing that the emperor was wearing his new clothes for all to see. As he rode by, some looked curiously at one another, a bit bewildered while others cheered and still others simply stared. But all of them, when asked, exclaimed, "What a fine set of clothes the emperor has! How proud he must be of his royal attire! He is splendid!" The parade continued.

But a little child in the crowd, who squinted and angled his head in an effort to see the emperor's new clothes, finally said right out loud: "The emperor isn't wearing any clothing."

Well, you can imagine the trouble that caused.

 ## Making It Mine

My brother Marty and I look alike. He's younger though. I was once teasing one my nieces and asked how she could tell us apart. She said that it was easy because "you have gray hair and he doesn't." I laughed. She continued, "And someday you'll be dead and he won't."

Telling the truth, that's the strength of youth. Unless we teach them otherwise, the young will say what they think, what they really think. What happens to the truth-telling as we move into the teen years and beyond? Mostly, what happens is self-doubt. We begin to believe that other people, all those "important" people, know better than we do. We doubt ourselves.

The bottom line is that the crowd will most often be cheering for the wrong thing. And if you're going to have the guts to stand up in the crowd and say the really hard thing, you'll need a lot of practice in all the little truths every day. Heroes aren't created overnight. Before their big moment they go about life doing all the little things in a heroic way. Here's a place to start: when the emperor is naked, say so. Trust yourself.

Prayer Starter

The Lord is my strength and my shield;
my heart trusts in him, and I am helped.
My heart leaps for joy and I will give thanks to him in song.

Psalm 28:7

I can do everything through him who gives me strength.

Philippians 4:13

God, I'll start with the small things. Every day show me when truth is being treated lightly or ignored completely. Let it be clear to me and give me the courage and confidence to speak up.

Soul Writing

Have you ever kept silent when something inside of you wanted to disagree with the popular opinion? Why did you fail to speak up? Think about another time when you or someone else said the unpopular thing. What happened? What thing is happening in your life right now about which you need to speak the truth?

14
God Wearing Skin

Something to Think About

In the fall of 1999 a man believed to be a prophet appeared in Hazelton, Pennsylvania. He was barefoot, wearing a white robe, had long hair and a beard. Residents say the gloom has lifted in the coal-mine town, and local priests say the pews are more jammed than they've ever been. One priest says he's seeing people he hasn't seen in twenty years. The local doctors say people are healing faster.

The prophet looks like a storybook picture of Jesus. People say he has a twinkle in his eye and he listens intently to others. Although he calls himself "What's His Name," his real name is Carl Joseph, and he's thirty-nine years old. In the last nine years he's wandered through thirteen countries and forty-seven states. He owns nothing but what he wears and he lives with whoever opens his door to him. He walks because it makes him accessible, he says.

We want someone
who listens and
who touches us and
who is with us.

He's been arrested in Ohio for refusing to break up a crowd of teenagers who gathered around him.

Carl models his life after Christ. He has never claimed to be Jesus; he has never claimed to be anything but a Christian telling others about Jesus. He is a traditional Catholic. He wants people to follow the rules, respect the Church, and live as faithful Catholics. People of all faiths flock to him when he's in a town. As many as two thousand have shown up at one of his town meetings. He talks about love and God's grace. And everywhere he goes, people report that their lives are changed.

Making It Mine

It's not hard to figure out that people respond to Carl Joseph because they view him as a living icon of Jesus. They know he isn't Jesus. But he walks into their towns and, in the image he presents, the story of God's love poured into the human man Jesus is portrayed right in front of them. We know Jesus' face, as depicted by artists, from all the storybooks and pictures. People want Jesus to be among us. So they respond to this man they call "the prophet" from whatever story of Jesus they have known or heard all their lives.

We want someone who listens and who touches us and who is with us. Regardless of your opinion of this wanderer, Carl Joseph's popularity is evidence of the human hunger to touch what is holy and divine.

Concerning this human hunger, there's a story about a child who isn't feeling well. He talks to his mother over the telephone while she's at work. She tells him that she loves him and that Jesus is with him when she can't be. The child responds, "But, Mommy, I want someone in skin."

The good news is that God did exactly that when Jesus came among us. God came in skin. Carl Joseph is dressing up like Jesus but can never be Jesus; the Christ was not God dressed up like a man. Jesus was actually a human being and actually God. Not one or the other, not almost one and not quite the other. He was fully, absolutely both. That's what we call mystery.

 # Prayer Starter

Your attitude should be the same as that of Christ Jesus:
Who, being in very nature God,
did not consider equality with God something to be
   grasped,
but made of himself nothing,
taking the very nature of a servant,
being made in human likeness.

Philippians 2:5-7

Lord Jesus, it is hard for me to understand how you can be both God and human. How you can completely be both. I guess that's what faith is for. Your life made the most difference on this planet than any life ever has. I will pay attention to your life and I will follow.

 Soul Writing

What difference does having "a God in skin" make to you personally? What do you think that means? How does it impact your life? Write a letter to Jesus about how it feels to be you.

15
Hypocrites in Church

Something to Think About

Simon, a young African-American man, describes an encounter he had with hypocrisy. "When I was in grammar school, I became a Reader of the Bible in church. One of the nuns said, 'You speak well. Why don't you read on Sunday?' So I became a Scripture reader. By the time I was in high school, I was still doing reading duties on Sundays, but now I got to hang around after church with the big guys.

"One day, I was standing outside the church and the pastor was standing outside with a couple of members of the Holy Name Society. They were talking about the impending closing of a parish school a few blocks away. Just beyond this parish was an African-American community, and some of the kids that lived in that neighborhood went to that other school. So, speaking out loud what he was thinking, the pastor turned around and spoke to these men, saying, 'Well, if they think those niggers are gonna come to our school, they've got another think coming.'

"And I was standing there thinking that these were the things that went on while I was in school, subtle little hints you get, these offhand remarks that you try to accept, because you get them all day, every day. You try to pass the whole thing off. But here was the guy wearing the collar, my pastor, the guy who said, 'Love thy neighbor,' and all these other things. What happened to all those lessons he gave on Sundays? All those things just came crashing down.

"In one instant, in one sentence, everything about church, everything about God, everything about loving everybody else was all rendered meaningless with one sentence. One sentence. This man was my pastor, my confessor, my friend . . . and he destroyed all of that with just one word — with the one word I thought I'd never hear a priest utter. I refused to go back to church.

"Once when some Mexican-American families asked that priest if they could have a Mexican guitar Mass in Spanish he said, 'Over my dead body.' Well, he's dead now and they have Spanish Mass there.

Nothing changes
unless you stay and
push back the
darkness.

"At his wake I went back to that church for the first time. I knelt there and couldn't think of anything to pray. I had written the church out of my life and was empty inside. Then, I realized that it was wrong of me to leave. I should be trying to change things."

From a story related at a retreat for young people

 ## Making It Mine

How many times have you heard people say, "I don't go to church because so many of the people are hypocrites"? What kind of sense does that make? Where do hypocrites belong if not in church? More importantly, what does it have to do with whether or not you are in church, or whether or not you are involved in doing something else worthwhile? Do you stay out of family functions because of hypocrites? How about movies? Do you avoid certain restaurants where hypocrites are known to gather for lunch? What about the beaches, malls, and concerts where hypocrites go?

There will always be hypocrites. Jesus had to deal with them and he was not particularly gentle with them. His strongest words are used against those who cover their selfish motives, bigotries, and greed in religious clothing. But it didn't keep Jesus out of religious gatherings. It didn't keep him from praying and it didn't cause him to abandon the whole bunch.

Jesus knew what the young man who tells the story above found out in the end. Someone else's hypocrisy is a thin excuse for walking away. Nothing changes unless you stay and push back the darkness.

That's what Jesus did. It cost him plenty. You know the story. So what are you going to do, make a lot of noise about those blasted hypocrites? That's easy — you hardly need a brain for that kind of complaining. Do more than that. Do what Simon did: try to change things.

Prayer Starter

I hate double-minded men,
but I love your law.
You are my refuge and my shield;
I have put my hope in your word.

Psalm 119:113-114

Faithful God, don't let me despair at hypocrisy. Instead, teach me to carefully guard myself from hypocrisy. Teach me to be as true as I possibly can. Teach me to say what I mean and live according to the values I claim are important. Don't let me add to the darkness.

Soul Writing

Put yourself in Simon's place. Imagine that it is you, your family, your friends the priest speaks of with hatred. Rather than leaving, what would you do?

16
Desert Graffiti

Something to Think About

In this excerpt, an ancient sacred ground of Native Americans was discovered while developers prepared to build a subdivision. The work was stopped so that archaeologists could review the stories and designs on cliffs and in caves.

Then came the pickups, 4x4's, jacked up and with chrome roll bars and double rows of spotlights. . . . Hundreds of symbolic designs intricately carved by Indian hunters, storytellers, shamans, and astronomers were power-chiseled . . . right off the cliff sides. Some of the vandals took potshots at the faces they saw there: the penetrating eyes, the lithe shapes of prancing bucks, the dancing outlines of masked figures. Some guilt no doubt remained in the vandals' genes. . . . Their shots revealed the hidden need to do away with even the slightest trace of the people their forefathers had slain as Europe colonized the American West. . . .

If we don't find our lives in some greater story than our own, we eventually lose our lives to some story lesser than our own.

"It's graffiti, that's all. Just like the graffiti we have on city buildings and underpasses in our own culture. 'Cept their culture is gone. Why preserve scribbles from a bunch of disappeared people that don't have anything to do with us?" That's how an enraged realtor described the Anasazi culture and its contribution to Native American rock art, an expression as unique and original as anything preserved in The Museum of Modern Art or in the great anthropological museums of Paris and Mexico City. . . . Frustrated that his land should be considered for purposes other than development, and the slowness of the archaeological study, the man hired a heavy-equipment operator to dislodge the boulders. In the middle of the night they were lifted into a truck, sacred etchings and all, and dumped in front of the Albuquerque city hall. This brazen statement was applauded by other developers, even though the man was cited, the boulders hauled back to their original site, and the property put under restriction. . . .

"You worship indoors, we worship outdoors. Would you approve of a bulldozer cutting through a corner of St. Patrick's or the Vatican to make way for frame-and-stucco houses? Do you think we approve the bulldozing of land that is sacred to us, that breathes with our ancestors' presence?" This was stated by one Native American representative during the controversy.

The inconsiderate hobbyists who loot prehistoric sites and the vandals who fire bullets at artistic, religious, or architectural monuments, whether cathedrals or kivas, are of the same breed who refuse kinship with cultures outside their own. Possessed of a volatile, short-wick egocentricity, they exhibit a disconnectedness that okays the decimation of one people's past for the sake of a newcomer's present. Or, of one man's running over another's family for diversion or self-preservation.

From *In the Desert We Do Not Count the Days*
by John Brandi

 # Making It Mine

All of us make sense of our lives according to some story we are part of. It might be the story of our family or it might be the story of our culture, but it is the story that we enter. The story existed before us and it shapes our lives. If we don't find our lives in some greater story than our own, we eventually lose our lives to some story lesser than our own.

The Bible is the story in which we find our lives, as Christians. It is the story of our Hebrew ancestors of faith and our Christian history, culture, and families.

Poet Desmond Egan has stated that our culture has witnessed the death of metaphor. You might be experiencing the result of this loss if you are, right now, having a difficult time understanding what it means to be part of a "story." That's a metaphor. Religious imagery is filled with metaphor. As a result, dying to metaphor means religious imagery becomes empty.

Is there any connection between this world as you experience it and an eternal realm of justice, goodness, beauty, and truth? The purpose of Scripture is to invite us into this realm; it is to connect us to this realm. Scripture shows us how this realm is relevant, but it shows us, largely, with metaphor. A fundamentalist approach to Scripture, or to life in general, is an impoverished, fragmented, lonely life. It is a life stripped of beauty and truth.

We can live our lives like the vandals who rip off sacred images, blind to their meaning and significance, or we can sit with the images and allow the images to tell us something about ourselves and our world. This is what Bible study is all about. This is why we listen to Scripture during Mass. We can allow the metaphor and the word of truth in Scripture to work on us or we can take ignorant potshots at it and try to bulldoze it out of our plans.

 # Prayer Starter

Your word is a lamp to my feet
and a light for my path.

Psalm 119:105

Lord, is there wisdom and guidance for me in Scripture? Will I find ancient, time-tested knowledge that applies to my wild world? Seems like a lot to ask of a story. Open my heart, and give me ears that hear.

Soul Writing

What has been your experience of Bible reading and study? Are you comfortable reading Scripture? Do you need help to understand it? Pick several lines from the Bible and rewrite them in your own words. Try these: Psalm 102:1-5; Isaiah 5:20-21; Matthew 15:16-20; 1 Timothy 4:12-14; 1 John 3:1-2.

17
Humble Like a Sparrow

Something to Think About

A teacher of spirituality asked us to define humility. The best the class could do was mention a few images. Humility is more like a sparrow than a peacock; humility resembles a small pond, not the majesty of the ocean; humility might be found in a vigil light rather than in the brilliance of a huge stained-glass window.

What is humility? It is that habitual quality whereby we live in the truth of things; the truth that we are creatures and not the Creator; the truth that our life is a composite of good and evil, light and darkness; the truth that in our littleness we have been given extravagant dignity. . . . Humility is truth: recognized, accepted, and embraced.

From *Humility: 31 Reflections on Christian Virtue*
by Robert F. Morneau

Making It Mine

What is humility? It is that habitual quality whereby we live in the truth of things. . . . Humility is truth: recognized, accepted, and embraced.

Reporters and VIP's were gathered at a Chicago train station to greet one of the most important men of the era. It was 1953, and the arrival of the 1952 Nobel Peace Prize winner was about to happen. He stepped off the train. A large man, he was well over six feet with a thundering presence, a head of wild, thick hair, and a bushy mustache. He seemed to fill the place as he stepped into the railroad station.

The place went crazy. People rushed toward the icon of brilliance and goodness. Reporters hurled questions at him, camera bulbs flashed, officials pressed close to shake his hand. He smiled and thanked everyone but seemed to be noticing a woman who had been on the train with him, a small elderly black woman. He said, "Excuse me just a moment," and moved through the crowd, past the crowd, heading toward the woman who was buckled under the weight of a huge suitcase.

He picked the bag up with one of his giant-sized hands, then put his hand under the woman's elbow. As he escorted her to a bus he talked softly, with his head stooped down to hers. They chatted a few more minutes, then he wished her a safe journey. Meanwhile the crowd moved a little closer, watching him. When she was on the bus he turned to them and said, "Sorry to have kept you waiting."

The man was Dr. Albert Schweitzer, famous doctor-missionary, follower of Christ who had spent his life serving the poor and dying in Africa. As he walked by, one member of the reception party turned to another and said, "That's the first time I ever saw a sermon walk."

Humility doesn't mean humiliation. It doesn't mean you stand still for others demeaning you. It doesn't mean you deny your gifts and talents. It just means that you know the truth about yourself. You know who you are; you know who you aren't. Because you know that, you become something we rarely find in this day and age. You become genuinely free. Kind of like a sparrow. The nice thing about being a sparrow is that you can rest assured God always knows where you are.

Prayer Starter

. . . It is good for me to be near God,
I have made the Sovereign Lord my refuge;
I will tell of all your deeds.

Psalm 73:28

Lord, help me to remember that I'm not the center of the universe. I am magnificent because you made me, but I am not God. Give me joy in being just what I am and accepting all the wonder of my gifts as well as my limits.

 **Soul Writing**

Imagine yourself at the train station, eagerly waiting for a famous, important person to arrive. Someone you admire deeply. How would you respond to that person doing what Schweitzer did? Write out your own definition for what humility means.

18
Growing Pains

Something to Think About

I knew the hour had come for me to move on to a place in life I had never been before.

And now I stand with waves at my feet and words spoken on a hillside two thousand years ago blowing like spindrift through my brain.

"Consider the lilies of the field, how they grow. . . ."

How they grow! There's the nub, that phrase tucked in so innocently, which we so easily overlook. I wonder how stunted I would be today if I were so worried about what I would eat, or what I would drink, or what I wear that I never dared venture. . . .

From *Beach Combing at Miramar: The Quest for an Authentic Life* by Richard Bode

Making It Mine

You stand on the brink of something new, growing up. It's a scary time sometimes. It's a wondrous time. Remember what Jesus said — and keep growing.

You'd never know it to look at me, but there are actually tall people in my family. All males, but tall nonetheless. Then, again, anyone six feet or taller seems pretty big to me. My oldest brother, Harry, always seemed tall to me.

I remember our mother rubbing his legs and ankles because she said, "He's having growing pains."

She said that sometimes he grew so fast the pants that he wore on Monday didn't fit him on Saturday. I didn't envy him all that growth, mostly because it meant growing pains that sounded like something terrible. I imagined a tree trying to break through crusty ground, pushing and wincing it's way through the tough soil, stretching itself painfully and reaching for the sunshine. Nice picture, but it sounded painful.

See how they grow, that's what Jesus said of the lilies. Look around you and notice that living things grow. They don't stay the same. They go from being one thing, to being another thing, even though they remain substantially the same thing. A lily is a lily even when it's just a seed and when there's no blossom. But the seed and the blossom don't look anything alike.

You stand on the brink of something new, growing up. It's a scary time sometimes. It's a wondrous time. Remember what Jesus said — and keep growing. It will probably hurt sometimes. Don't be afraid of growing pains though. You can count on God to be with you; you can count on your family and on your real friends. Don't let worry about what's going to happen to you or what the future holds keep you from beholding the lilies, and growing with them.

Prayer Starter

Remain in me and I will remain in you.
No branch can bear fruit by itself; it must remain in the vine.
Neither can you bear fruit unless you remain in me.
I am the vine; you are the branches.

John 15:4-5a

Lord, my spirit and body strains with all the changes. Nothing is ever the same for very long; I am especially not the same as I was last month or last week or yesterday. In all this growing I want to grow toward you.

Soul Writing

How have you changed in the last year? Try to imagine how you will be in a year, five years, ten years. Write about your growing pains and write a prayer of your own asking God to help you with the growing pains.

19
First Class All the Way to the Wrong Place

Something to Think About

A few years ago Mark Lowry, Tony Wood, and I wrote a song called "First Class, Wrong Flight." It's about a man who is given a first-class ticket, but it's for the wrong flight.

Sure, he's traveling in style. He's in the company of CEO's, VIP's, and movie stars. His dinner is being served on real china instead of in a cardboard box. He's got all the good magazines, a recliner seat, and unlimited beverages (served in crystal instead of plastic cups). His every desire is being met. There's only one problem. He's not going where he wants to go.

Unfortunately, some of us are traveling through life that way. We're doing it in style, making sure our every desire is being met. We rub shoulders with the elite, the "in" crowd, as we fly from place to place. But we're traveling in the wrong direction, going where the world wants us to go, instead of following the path God has for us. What's the point of all the luxury, of lookin' good, if, when we reach the end of our journey, we're nowhere near the place God wanted us to be?

In all the planning and all the dreaming, have you given any thought to where God is in the whole plan?

From *Don't Jump to Conclusions Without a Bungee Cord and Other Wise Advice: Devotions for Teens From the Book of Proverbs* by Martha Bolton

Making It Mine

Maybe the future is all laid out for you. You've picked a great college. You know where you want to work, the kind of house you'll buy. You know what you'll do with your life and you are ready to head into the life you've been planning and dreaming of. You've worked hard for all of it.

There's nothing wrong with good plans or owning things or having good things. The problem is that "things" get in the way; they distract you from the goal, where you are supposed to be going.

In all the planning and all the dreaming, have you given any thought to where God is in the whole plan? The thing about God is that he's a lot like a dandelion. He tends to show up in our tame and perfect landscapes just when we least expect it. God is the unknown factor in your future. Unknown, but faithful. Unknown and able to delight you with surprise. All you have to do is include God. It's not complicated. When you're making plans — pray. Pray and listen.

Plan your life, dream your dreams. But don't forget to include God in the big picture. Otherwise, you might just end up in first class headed for the wrong place.

 ## Prayer Starter

You are my portion, O Lord;
I have promised to obey your words.
I have sought your face with all my heart;
be gracious to me according to your promise.
I have considered my ways
and have turned my steps to your statutes.

Psalm 119:57-59

Father, I can conceive of wondrous plans and imagine a life exactly suited for me. But I can't imagine it without you. I know you'll never leave me. I want to make sure I never leave you. Guide me. Keep me on track.

Soul Writing

What can you do to consciously include God in your future? Imagine that God is telling you what wonderful things are ahead for you. Write it down.

20
Afraid of the Big Bad Wolf

Something to Think About

Author Robin R. Meyers, in Morning Sun on a White Piano, *writes of his toddler son Blue's passion for "bunny" stories and how he discovers his son is adamantly against the appearance of evil.*

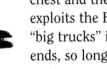

We can't keep the evil from springing out of the bushes, but we can turn to God for comfort, strength, change, and safety.

. . . We pile on the couch, Blue squats cross-legged on my chest and the unrehearsed tales begin. It doesn't matter what exploits the Bunny may encounter, so long as there are a few "big trucks" in the story and it doesn't matter how the story ends, so long as Bunny is triumphant. But one thing does matter very much: the Wolf, that first acquaintance with evil every child makes in reading "The Three Little Pigs."

What I discover that morning is that Blue is strenuously opposed to the appearance of the Wolf in any other story, especially as a threat to his beloved Bunny. . . . I decide to liven up an otherwise floundering Bunny story with a little Wolf attack. "Out of the woods he comes, the wicked old Wolf, and grabs the Bunny!"

"No Wolf! No Wolf!" shouts Blue, his face etched with a concern too deep for skin like his. The brows drop, the eyes grow bright, and he reaches to cover my mouth with his tiny hand. . . . I try some crude foreshadowing: "The Bunny will win, Blue, believe me. . . ." That doesn't work. I even offer to send the monster back into the woods. . . . This doesn't work either . . . it isn't good enough. Blue wants him out of the story. . . .

In his world, free from harm, there is no need to look over your shoulder. The sound of footsteps meant the approach of a friend. . . .

From *Morning Sun on a White Piano: Simple Pleasures and the Sacramental Life* by Dr. Robin R. Meyers

Making It Mine

One of the hardest times for parents is the moment when their child comes face to face with evil. It might be the bully on the bus or the cousin who hits for no reason; sadly for many children innocence is lost to violence and cruelty we can hardly imagine.

Ancient Celtic Christians believed that God was present in the smallest events of their lives. They believed that God cared about their slightest fears, their largest joys, and everything in between. At the same time, the prayers that have emerged from their tradition deal unflinchingly with the problem of evil. That doesn't mean they found the answer to the question. But in the prayers they have left us we find a realistic view of fear and suffering. We also find hope.

We can't keep the Wolf out of the story. Close your eyes and wish it with all your heart, wolves will show up sooner or later. However, just as the old fairy tales give us a place to first hear the story of evil and learn that it moves among us, the ancient Celtic prayers give us words with which to speak of suffering and pain. We can't keep the evil from springing out of the bushes, but we can turn to God for comfort, strength, change, and safety.

Prayer Starter

The Lord watches over you;
the Lord is your shade at your right hand;
the sun will not harm you by day,
nor the moon by night.
The Lord will keep you from all harm;
he will watch over your life;
the Lord will watch over your coming and going
both now and forevermore.

Psalm 121:5-8

An ancient Celtic prayer:
Empty and bereft I be
I cry to Thee;
Mother me.

Angry and afraid I be,
I long for Thee;
Father me.

Slighted and alone I be,
I reach for Thee;
Stay with me.

Grieving and in pain I be,
You come to me;
Explain to me.

You feel for me;
You weep for me;
Redeeming me;
Releasing me.

Soul Writing

Write about a time when you experienced God taking care of you. Write about a time when you were aware of the Wolf and your vulnerability. How do you cope with fear and your sense of vulnerability? What might help you cope better or differently?

21
How to Be Great

Something to Think About

What makes a person great? According to the Backstreet Boys you're larger than life when you love and realize the power of your love to shape not only yours but the larger reality. That's the message of their song "Larger Than Life." It's not bad theology for a boy band.

Ricky Byrdsong was a great man. You might recognize his name — he was a basketball coach. He once got disgusted with his Big Ten team and went up into the bleachers to sit with the spectators. He wasn't a great coach, but we're not talking about being a great coach, or postal worker, or parent. Ricky Byrdsong was a great man.

He worked hard in the Chicago area to help African-American kids go for their dreams. Kids, that's what he cared about. He taught them to respect themselves and he taught them to turn away from bigotry.

Which makes it more than slightly ironic that Ricky Byrdsong was gunned down by a militant bigot as Ricky's children watched. After Ricky's death the people in his neighborhood took nightly walks of the same route Ricky and his children had taken. All of them together: Christian and Jew, black and white, young and old. They walked together, sending the message that Ricky's death had not been in vain. They had heard his message and they would carry on his work. Ricky inspired other people to great things; that's what made Ricky Byrdsong a great human being.

Greatness refuses to play the power games of who is winning and who is losing, who is the powerful and who is the powerless. Jesus is the model for this kind of greatness.

Making It Mine

Greatness refuses to play the power games of who is winning and who is losing, who is the powerful and who is the powerless. Jesus is the model for this kind of greatness. There is a story most you have probably heard about John and Sandy.

John and Sandy are close friends. They have been friends for a lifetime and one day John says to Sandy, "You and I have never had an argument."

"That's true we haven't," she replies.

"Well, maybe we should try to be like everyone else — let's have an argument."

"What will we argue over?"

"I've seen how it works. We'll get a brick and one of us will hold it and say to the other, 'This is my brick, you cannot have it.' The other one replies, 'No, it is my brick and you have taken it from me, give it back.' Then we argue."

"Okay," she agrees. "You go first."

And so John picks up a brick and says, "This brick is mine!"

Sandy sighs deeply and says gently, "Well, John, if it's your brick, take it."

And so they are unable to argue.

But as long as we clutch at bricks and speak of mine and yours we will continue to argue. These little power games grow into huge power games and those grow into wars and worlds come apart and people are shattered because we won't give up the brick in our hand. Men like Ricky Byrdsong die because of it.

 # Prayer Starter

Those who trust in the Lord are like Mount Zion,
which cannot be shaken but endures forever.

Psalm 125:1

The Lord is with me; I will not be afraid.
What can man do to me?

Psalm 118:6

Great God, there will be achievements and failures in my life. I will wrestle for great things and I will settle for less sometimes. But whatever I do, keep my mind clear and my heart true. Remind me often of what it means to be great.

Soul Writing

What does greatness mean to you? What great things would you like to do with your life? Write a few paragraphs about the characteristics of a genuinely great person. When you think of greatness, who is the first person who comes to mind? Why?

22
Living in the Land of Violence

Something to Think About

When I was six years old, my parents gave me a rifle for Christmas. It was a popgun, which they considered harmless, which is why they bought it for me. What they hadn't counted on was a boy's capacity to turn even the most innocuous object into an instrument of violence. While it was true that the gun couldn't fire bullets, it did make one heck of a club, which I learned while engaging my brother in hand-to-hand combat.

Shortly after that, my mother grew concerned about war toys and wouldn't buy us any more guns. That was fine with us, since by then we had discovered football. Mr. Smitherman was my football coach. I don't remember much about him, except that he was always yelling at us to kill the other team. That was on Saturdays. On Sundays he taught Sunday school, mostly stuff from the Old Testament about God smiting people.

All of this was done, of course, to prepare us guys for the "real" world, which would chew us up and spit us out if we weren't tough. What it actually did was turn us into insensitive brutes whose idea of entertainment was making body noises with our armpits.

From *Front Porch Tales* by Philip Gulley

Women are freeing themselves from the bondage of always pleasing others and men are freeing themselves from the bondage of being tough guys.

Making It Mine

Girls know it's true that boys tend to be less than civilized when left to themselves. Boys know it's true also. Over years of leading retreats for teens I've discovered that a retreat goes much better if there are girls present to keep the boys from becoming "insensitive brutes whose idea of entertainment was making body noises. . . ."

More and more though, boys aren't the only ones emulating the worse of masculine behavior. It is considered cool by many boys and girls to be insensitive, brash, and have an attitude. It isn't a macho thing anymore. For example, when talking to either gender about graphic violence in movies and video games it's common that some teens say they think only wimps would be disturbed by it. They express a definite pride in their failure to be moved by portrayals of horrific acts.

For a very long time our world has been considered a man's world. What that really means is a world where might and power are considered noble aspirations. It was a world spun by male values and that made it feminine to feel, to communicate, to cry, and to be a person of faith. Over the last couple of decades it's improved greatly for both genders. Women are freeing themselves from the bondage of always pleasing others and men are freeing themselves from the bondage of being tough guys.

Yet here we are with the old problem of people, both men and women, being insensitive to suffering. So maybe that's not a gender thing. Men and women after all are both from earth and it's a fine place. Instead of looking to simplistic gender theories for the answer to why people are growing increasingly violent and comfortable with violence, perhaps we should be looking at a couple of other factors.

1. Violent portrayals are common in music, television, and movies.

2. The violence has been around a long time, and the longer something is with us, the less we respond to it.

The crucifixion is an example. Christ's torture and death was nothing tender or pleasant. It was execution and torture. It was bloody. It smelled awful. It was raw. After some two thousand years of looking at it we have a nice sanitary crucifixion that has overwhelmingly lost its power to move people.

The situation is not a symptom of what's wrong with boys, or what is going wrong with girls. It is a symptom of a society that is choking on its own blood. We aren't going to offer a solution here. If you're waiting for that, well, it isn't going to happen. No simple Band-Aid is going to stop this bloody mess. You have the ability to make a difference by saying no. You don't need anyone to make the choice for you. You know very well when it is too much.

A friend talked about her Thanksgiving family gathering last year. There was a small child there, not yet two years old. Someone put a movie in the VCR just to keep the kids occupied while adults played cards and talked. So with the background noise of her parents laughing and her grandparents eating stuffing and playing rummy, the little girl watched her first murder. And then she took her bunny and went to bed.

Prayer Starter

This is what the Sovereign Lord says: You have gone far enough, . . . Give up your violence and oppression and do what is right.
Ezekiel 45:9a

God, the violent images are all around me. I'm not sure I am even aware of them most of the time. Everyone says it's not real and is harmless. Show me how I am influenced by the images. Show me where I have grown hard. Help me be honest with myself and with my friends. If change is going to happen, let it start with my generation.

 Soul Writing

How have violent portrayals in music, movies, videos, and television affected you? How have they impacted your friends? This month keep a log of the violent images you are subjected to. If you viewed this process through completely fresh eyes — say as an alien visiting our world — how would it seem to you?

23
What My Heart Already Knows

Something to Think About

All my life I've tried to find it
Searching for a reason and a rhyme
Though you've always led the way
I will still get lost sometimes
How could I be so blind?

But if I ever learn what my heart already knows
And not feel the hurt that I wear on my sleeve,
But the laughter that burns inside of my soul
Let the child come alive, and drive away those ghosts
You know my head ain't even close to what my heart
    already knows.

From My *Heart Already Knows* by Rick Elias,
Mark Robertson, and Rich Mullins

There are ancient places and ancient voices in your young heart. That's where you'll find God.

In the Bible, practically every organ in the body is mentioned except the brain. The ancient authors of Scriptures regarded the heart . . . as the seat of emotional as well as physical life . . . [and as the] monitor of conscience.

In ancient Egypt as well as Judea, the heart was regarded not only as the power of life but also as the source both of good and evil thoughts. In addition to the heart, the person was considered to have a shadow, a name, a double (a soul and a spirit). After death the shadow was lost, but the double, the soul and the spirit, remained. . . .

Millennia have passed since the era of Moses and Ramses, but to this day we employ the word "heart" to describe emotions and character. One is kindhearted, softhearted, fainthearted, or heartless. We call a beloved, sweetheart. On Valentine's Day, the heart becomes the symbol of love. Perhaps there is a lingering subconscious tribal memory that carries us back to a distant past as we accept the dictum "Thou shalt love the Lord with all thy heart."

From "Kallet's Column," by Herbert I. Kallet, M.D.,
in *Bulletin* magazine

Making It Mine

According to Paul Pearshall, Ph.D., author of *The Heart's Code*, the heart is the key to the soul. He says this goes beyond any sentimental ideas about the heart being what you give away on Valentine's Day. He means our actual, blood-pumping, pulsating physical organ. According to Dr. Pearshall, the heart has a kind of intelligence that receives certain sorts of signals and energy from the brain and that a large portion of these signals involve memory.

In other words, the heart remembers. There are things your heart knows, coded into your actual physical structure, which it has known for as long as you have had a heart.

It could well be what is responsible for the fact that everyone makes a choice about God. There is no person alive who does not face the question about what to do about God. Even if the choice ends up being that you will ignore God, or you decide that God doesn't exist, there is still the undeniable impulse to decide to do something about God.

The heart, in remembering, calls us back to what has always been, to what we know is true, to what is more than we thought we knew. It is this deeper intelligence that compels us to look for meaning and that determines, ultimately, what matters most for each of us. There are ancient places and ancient voices in your young heart. That's where you'll find God.

Prayer Starter

For . . . you knit me together in my mother's womb.
My frame was not hidden from you. . . .
When I was woven together in the depths of the earth,
your eyes saw my unformed body.
All the days ordained for me
were written in your book
before one of them came to be.

Psalm 139:13, 15-16

God, if there is a deeper intelligence in me, a place that can hear your voice, a place where the truth is obvious and things are generally more clear, I'd like to know about it. Help me be quiet enough to listen to my heart. Help me remember what I already know.

Soul Writing

Write about an experience you've had of hearing your own heart. Maybe you think of it as intuition or a "gut" feeling. What happened when you followed, or didn't follow, your heart? What keeps you from hearing this inner voice? What could you do to learn to listen better?

24
Face the Music

Something to Think About

You've heard the expression "Face the music." Have you ever wondered where the phrase comes from? Here's the story.

Many years ago a man wanted to play in the Imperial Orchestra; the only problem was that the man couldn't play a single note of music. He was, however, a person of immense wealth and influence, so he demanded that he be made part of the orchestra or he would withdraw his support and the orchestra would flounder.

The conductor agreed to let him sit in the second row of the orchestra, and even though he could not read music or play a flute, a flute was put into his hands. When a concert began he would raise it to his mouth and move his fingers. He never made a sound though. He went through the motions and many people didn't know the truth about him. The deception continued for a number of years. Until a new conductor took over the orchestra. He told the members of the orchestra that since he didn't know their work personally he wanted to hear each of them play individually.

It's never smart to pretend you're something other than what you are.

In this way he intended to weed out inferior musicians and help strengthen the genuinely gifted among them. One by one, each of the musicians performed for the new conductor. The fake flutist was naturally frantic that he'd be discovered. He had long thought his deception was accepted and unknown. So he pretended to be sick. However, no doctor would verify his illness. He made other excuses until finally the conductor said his time was up. He expected the "flutist" to take his instrument, sit with a sheet of music in front of him, and demonstrate his skill.

Sitting before the music, sitting in the silence, he had to "face the music." That was the day he discovered he could not hide any longer in the music made by others.

Making It Mine

It's never smart to pretend you're something other than what you are. All of us are tempted by our own insecurities.

We don't feel good enough. We don't feel smart enough, attractive enough, witty enough. The problem is that we compare ourselves to everyone else. When we compare, we'll always come up short. No two people are gifted the same way. No two people have the same history. No two people will respond to a situation in exactly the same way. You can know that intellectually and still struggle with comparing yourself to others.

Anne went to school with me briefly. She moved in from California in October and finished that year, then went to a private school during her junior year. We were sophomores together. Everything about Anne was just so cool. She had the bluest eyes I had ever seen and deep golden-colored hair plus a great wardrobe. She was funny and creative. She always had new ideas about what we could do next for excitement.

She asked me once how often I did my nails. I told her I did them daily, and after that she did hers every day too and mentioned it often. Another time she asked me where I met a group of friends after school. A couple of days later she showed up with a small group of girls. When I wore a purple dress that got a lot of attention, Anne had a red one in the same style within a couple of weeks. Little things? That's what I thought. I'm sure Anne was comparing herself to lots of the girls we hung out with. Anne and I weren't really close. I liked her and we did things now and then, talked on the phone, and had fun.

That winter, no one asked Anne to the Valentine's dance. A friend of mine, Don, wanted to, but he said he didn't dare approach "Queen Anne." It's hard to be new to a school and we figured the guys just needed more time to get to know her. I asked Anne to ride with four of us who were double-dating. It wasn't a serious kind of dating and we liked having her around. She declined and said her boyfriend, Ron, was visiting from California (much older boyfriend and in the Army) and she was planning to go to his parents' hunting cabin with him. Her parents knew and trusted Ron, so it was fine with them. We were all pretty impressed.

The next week she brought us a picture of Ron in his uniform. After that, she talked about him all the time. The two of them did incredible things like drive to Florida for a few days (she was fifteen at the time) and he was always buying things for her, things her parents wouldn't let her keep. He gave her a promise ring on her sixteenth birthday. And he managed to spend most weekends with her, since he had been stationed at a nearby military base. She never had time for the usual high-school events because she was dining at adult restaurants, going to cocktail parties, and cooking for his friends and their wives. You've probably guessed that she was lying.

Ron existed all right, but he was the son of a friend of the family — nothing more. I met him a year later. He was related to a boy I was dating. We were at a family reunion with him. I hadn't seen Anne since she started attending a private school. I asked him how Anne was doing and he said she was fine as far as he knew. I asked if they were still planning on getting married when Anne graduated next year. He looked baffled and said, "I never dated Anne. Anne is like my sister or little cousin, something like that. I've been dating Marie" — he motioned toward a petite girl-next-door type who was playing volleyball — "since I was fifteen. Where did you hear I was dating Anne?"

I never had the chance to ask Anne why she lied. Didn't need to. Obviously she wanted to impress us; she didn't want us to think that no one wanted to be with her. She didn't want us to think that she cared about our unimportant high-school events. Even though Anne wasn't present the day I found out the truth, I'm sure she eventually had to face the music, if not for that lie, then for another one. Anne wasn't happy with her life and so she created a different life for herself. Probably the life she thought would be wonderful. She probably liked Ron a great deal. And she envied those of us who had grown up together and were easy, warm friends. It had to be hard to come into our small town and be from California.

I wish Anne had not pretended. I think I would have liked the real Anne a whole lot. But the real Anne chose to remain a stranger to all of us.

 **Prayer Starter**

The Lord will fulfill his purpose for me;
your love, O Lord, endures forever —
do not abandon the works of your hands.

Psalm 138:8

Lord, in those moments when I am tempted to lift a mask to my face and pretend I am something other than what I am, remind me of what a gift it is to be exactly who I am. Help me remember that the truth is always enough.

Soul Writing

What would have caused Anne to make up the elaborate story? If you've ever been part of anything similar, write about what happened and how you felt. Are there things about yourself that you keep hidden or don't admit to? What do you think makes people hide behind masks?

25
Loving Like Ethel

Something to Think About

This is quoted from the novel A Perfect Storm *by Sebastian Junger. It's about a bar called the Crow's Nest and its owner, Ethel, who is like a mother to a herd of rough, odd, and difficult-to-like "orphans."*

One night at the bar a thin old man who had lost his niece to AIDS wrapped his arms around Ethel and just held on to her for five or ten minutes. At the other end of the spectrum is a violent little alcoholic named Wally who's a walking testimony to the effects of child abuse. He has multiple restraining orders against him and occasionally slides into realms of such transcendent obscenity that Ethel has to yell out to him to shut the hell up. She has a soft spot for him, though, because she knows what he went through as a child, and one year she wrapped up a present and gave it to him Christmas morning. (She's in the habit of doing that for anyone stuck upstairs over the holidays.) All day long Wally avoided opening it, and finally Ethel told him she was going to get offended if he didn't unwrap the damn thing. Looking a little uneasy, he slowly pulled the paper off; the gift was a scarf or something and suddenly the most violent man in Gloucester was crying in front of her.

Ethel, he said, shaking his head, no one's ever given me a present before.

One moment of kindness probably won't change any life but your own. Like prayer, kindness is going to rearrange you into a better person.

Making It Mine

There's an important line in the story about Ethel that most of us would read and not think about. "She has a soft spot for him . . . she knows what he went through as a child. . . ."

That doesn't mean Wally is excused for being mean and doing horrible things. It doesn't mean that anyone should ignore Wally's problems. Obviously, you wouldn't be doing Wally a favor if you did that. However, Ethel's simple act of human kindness provides us with a blinking glance at the real person Wally was created to be, the person he may never be because someone wounded him so badly.

A friend tells a story about the college campus on which he used to teach. It's a lovely campus dotted with ponds and lush green lawns. It also has a hardy flock of ducks that call it home and a woman known to faculty and students as the "Duck Woman" because she talks to the ducks, swears at the ducks, chases the ducks.

As he's leaving the campus one day this friend encounters the Duck Woman sitting on the grass, yelling at the ducks, but only slightly agitated. He says he doesn't know what got into him, but he sat beside her and said, "Hi. Isn't it a beautiful day? How are you doing?"

He looked into her eyes and he spoke to her as he would any "normal" person who doesn't yell at ducks on college campuses.

"She looked at me," he related, "with this wild, glazed look in her eyes and then, all of a sudden her eyes seemed to clear and her face relaxed and she was looking back at me with the expression of any normal woman. She said, 'Thank you for asking. No one ever does. I'm not so good but I'm used to it.' She turned her head back to the ducks and about fifteen seconds passed before she started yelling at the ducks again."

He was rattled by the experience. He had caught a glimpse of the woman, the real person whose name no one knew and so they called her the Duck Woman. Her lucid seconds haunt him even now when he's moved on and isn't teaching there and doesn't ever see her anymore. He says he knows she has "a story of wounding I can't even imagine." It's permanently changed how he looks at all the wounded people he encounters.

One moment of kindness probably won't change any life but your own. Like prayer, kindness is going to rearrange you into a better person. Chances are, that's the only result you'll ever see. There's no point pretending otherwise. Is it enough that the one moment of kindness you give someone else is one less moment of pain? What if, by some holy occurrence, those moments of kindness should string together, one person after another, one incidence of goodness after another? It's a place to start, and when you do what you can, well, who knows . . .

Prayer Starter

The Lord loves righteousness and justice;
the earth is full of his unfailing love.

Psalm 33:5

A new command I give you: Love one another. As I have loved you, so you must love one another. By this all men will know that you are my disciples, if you love one another.

John 13:34

Kind God, it is easy to look away from the ones who are most wounded, most different. It's harder to love some people. So much about them makes me uneasy. Give me a love that won't look away, a love like yours.

# Soul Writing

Describe an encounter you've had or observed with someone like Wally or the Duck Woman. Write honestly about your feelings and responses. Pay attention to how others react to those with handicaps, the homeless, and others who are different. What accounts for the way most people respond to these persons? What can you do to change your own responses? Make an effort to be a little kinder and write about the experience.

26
Chicken Soup for the Soul Is Not Enough

Something to Think About

A lot of people — young and otherwise, but especially those from, say, the mid-teens to mid-thirties — become disillusioned when they get the sneakers with lights in them, and they have the new avocado-salad shooter, and they have the jacket with Michael Jordan's picture on the back, and they realize that it's not enough. People wonder: What the hell? What's wrong here?

George Carlin in *Free Inquiry,* Summer 1999

We need something drastic, something that can actually make a change, a heart transplant; we need to be reshaped — we need conversion.

Psychologist Rollo May studied young women who had been rejected by their families at an early age. He was puzzled to discover that many of them were well-adjusted and emotionally healthy with a strong sense of personal worth. May said what he discovered is that it was not rejection by a mother that crushed the human spirit. Those who have been openly and frankly rejected usually went out and created another family for themselves. They did this by connecting to others and forming an intimate circle of relationships. The people who rejected them made no bones about it: they knew those they rejected would have to look for love and affirmation elsewhere.

The persons who are traumatized by rejection, May conjectured, are those who are rejected but who are lied to about it. In other words, the real trauma happens to a person's emotional health when a mother or other close person tells the child she loves him or her when in fact that person is incapable of giving love or possibly feeling love. The words and the actions don't match, so the child never comes to know or understand the world in which they must live. They can't orient themselves or acclimate to their own existence.

Making It Mine

We know we're in trouble. We sense that we're being lied to and that's why we can't get oriented to our existence. This fact accounts for the popularity of the *Chicken Soup for the Soul* books. A lot of people, especially teens, have been inspired by these books and that's a good thing. But it is not a permanent cure for our souls. Our souls need more than chicken soup.

We need something drastic, something that can actually make a change, a heart transplant; we need to be reshaped — we need conversion. This is the gospel of Jesus, that Jesus entered the human condition, got into the mud with us so that we could be led out of that soul-crushing muck.

St. Patrick is a good guide for us in days like these. Writing of him in *How the Irish Saved Civilization*, Thomas Cahill says, "To him, no less than to them (the Irish), the world is full of magic. . . . The difference between Patrick's magic and the magic of the druids is that in Patrick's world all beings and events come from the hand of a good God, who loves human beings and wishes them success. . . ."

The magical world is not filled with dread or lies. Rather, because Christ is in every flower, every rock, and every snowflake, it is charged with the shining of God; the Word of God speaks on every breeze and calls you in the rapids and whirlwinds.

We don't need chicken soup as much as we need to listen, to believe, and to know that we are the children of God and, though seemingly stranded on this wet chunk of rock called earth, we are not, cannot, ever be alone.

Prayer Starter

Though the mountains be shaken
and the hills be removed,
yet my unfailing love for you
will not be shaken.

Isaiah 54:10a

*Lord, the lies of the culture, the confusion of the crowd —
these get into my soul sometimes and I get very, very lost.
Come to me in all the magical ways that you do. Startle me
into the strength and rest of your enfolding care.*

 Soul Writing

Name ways the culture and media state things that aren't completely true. Since we're always having to sort the truth from the lies, how does that impact the human spirit? How could a closer relationship with God help you sort through it all?

27
What Arthur Miller Wanted to Tell Marilyn Monroe

Something to Think About

Few people in the latter half of the twentieth century have provoked public fascination and imagination as much as Marilyn Monroe. . . . She has become, I think, a kind of mythological figure, a symbol of our time — restless, hungering for love, unrestrained self-indulgence, bitter unfulfillment, tragic death.

During Marilyn's childhood her mother was institutionalized, and because there was no other place Marilyn could stay, she was taken to an orphanage. When she realized what was happening, she dug in her heels and yelled, "But I'm not an orphan! I'm not an orphan!" She was correct, in the factual sense, but ever after she felt like one and seems to have spent much of her life running from that feeling. She sought desperately to prove to the world and to herself that she wasn't unwanted, that she wasn't alone. . . .

One of the men to whom she ran was Arthur Miller, the brilliant New York playwright. The world wondered at the strange combination of this marriage: Jewish intellectual with a back-slidden-Fundamentalist sex kitten. But there was more to the relationship than might have been apparent. . . . During the filming of *The Misfits*, Miller watched Marilyn's descent into the depths of depression. . . . He feared for her life. . . . One evening after a doctor had been persuaded to give her still another shot, she fell asleep. Miller stood watching her, reflecting.

"I found myself straining to imagine miracles," he wrote. "What if she were to wake and I were to say, 'God loves you, darling,' and she were to believe it! How I wished I still had my religion and she still had hers. . . . I had no saving mystery to offer her."

From *Finding Happiness in the Most Unlikely Places* by Donald McCullough

The Church and our families impart to us a saving mystery. The truths we are given, the sacraments by which we are saved — these are valuable treasure.

Making It Mine

Listen to a parable about a young man who is given an ancient and beautiful family ring when he leaves home to attend college. This giving of a ring is his culture's tradition. The ring is more than jewelry, it is the family crest. The boy's history and goals are represented by the ring. It epitomizes his identity.

At school he soon discovers that his family ring is not like the rings the other kids are wearing. What his family has given him is different. The other kids at school have rings all right, but newer ones, all more or less alike — none of them like his. The difference makes him feel like he'll never belong. He grows ashamed of the difference and eventually hides the ring, replacing it with a snazzy trendy titanium one that looks like the other kids' rings. He immediately feels better about himself and settles in for the remainder of his first year away from home.

When it's time to go home he realizes he needs to find the ring. But he doesn't know where it is. He has forgotten, completely. He realizes he will have to return home with the cheap, trendy one. He hopes his family and friends won't notice. As he walks toward home and away from the crowd at school the titanium ring starts looking trashy. He can't believe he gave up the real thing for a trendy counterfeit. He realizes that even if he can deceive his family, he'll always know the truth. He knows that he will spend all his life looking for what he lost.

Just in case you've missed the point, he had the "saving mystery" but chose a counterfeit. It is the story of our lives. It is the story of the prodigal son. It is the story of how all of us set out to find what is lost. Musician Billy Joel wrote it this way, "I'm looking for something, something sacred I lost . . . and it can only be seen by the eyes of the blind. . . ."

The Church and our families impart to us a saving mystery. The truths we are given, the sacraments by which we are saved — these are valuable treasure. That's not always easy to understand or grasp. It makes for a sad life when we spend our days chasing what we once had and foolishly gave up.

Prayer Starter

Be merciful to me, O God, be merciful,
for I have taken refuge in you;
in the shadow of your wings will I take refuge
until this time of trouble has gone by.

Psalm 57:1

Lord Jesus, when I think I can handle my life alone — remind me that I'm wrong. When I want to hide myself from others or I settle for the easy and cheap, stop me. When my actions will hurt others — protect me from such actions. Show me what matters most.

 **Soul Writing**

Think about the phrase "saving mystery." Do you need to be rescued? From what? What "mystery" saves? What does it mean to call the cross of Christ a saving mystery? Write about this.

28
Rock 'n' Roll: The Story of Redemption?

Something to Think About

The story of the Gospel is told night after night in one of the least likely places: VH1, the cable station that boasts "Music First." Night after night they tell the stories of rock stars. John Mellencamp. Cher. Billy Joel. Rod Stewart. Donna Summers. Bruce Springstein. They are the stuff legends are made of. Their lives are also good illustrations of a term you might have heard in church — redemption.

Everyone dreams; everyone goes after those dreams.

Joseph Campbell, expert on mythology, has stated that celebrities are the equivalent of Greece's many gods. They can be in more than one place at once; even if they die, they live on, and we see their image, hear their words. But just in case we start taking this god-thing of the stars too seriously, along comes VH1 to remind us that their stories are often tragic stories. Tragic, but there is always this twist at the end, a moment of grace, a coming of age, a slow light that brings the aging rock star into a collision with the ego that is self.

The story is only slightly different for each one; always it is the story of struggles and the rise to fame, the crescendo and, then, the fall. There is always the fall. Life is like that. You've probably heard some say that VH1 tells the same story over and over. It's true. And it's comforting. Because that is our story. This rising, falling, growing, and becoming better for it: this is the story of what it is to be human and what it is to be part of a people redeemed by a God who is determined to love us into life.

Making It Mine

Maybe our stories aren't all that different from those of mythic gods, rock stars, and the kid down the street. When you look closely enough, there are more similarities than differences. Everyone dreams; everyone goes after those dreams. To some degree we all make the dreams our own; we persevere until we have the life we carve out for ourselves. And when we are at ease we realize that it isn't enough.

I denied myself nothing my eyes desired;
I refused my heart no pleasure.
My heart took delight in all my work,
and this was the reward for all my labor.
Yet when I surveyed all that my hands had done
and what I had toiled to achieve,
everything was meaningless, a chasing after the wind;
nothing was gained under the sun.

Ecclesiastes 2:10-11

These words are reputed to have been written by one of the richest men who ever lived. Think of him surrounded by his riches, his harem, his luxury — and yet, with all the wealth he could accumulate, something inside of him remained hungry and empty; wealth wasn't enough, wasn't the answer.

There is a God-shaped hole inside of you. If you haven't discovered this hungering void inside of you, wait awhile, because it will get your attention. You can stuff it with all the best and it won't be filled. You are made to walk at God's side. Only God can give peace. Ask an old rock star.

Prayer Starter

You have filled my heart with greater joy
than when their grain and new wine abound.
I will lie down and sleep in peace,
for you alone, O Lord,
make me dwell in safety.

Psalm 4:7-8

Peace I leave with you; my peace I give you. I do not give to you as the world gives. Do not let your hearts be troubled and do not be afraid.

John 14:27

Lord Jesus, if there's anything that is hard to come by it is peace. You call me to rest; you call me to peace. Lord, here I am. I'll take the peace.

Soul Writing

Whom do you know who seems to be peaceful? Write about that person. What about that person gives you the impression of peacefulness? Talk to that person to find out how he or she has come to be peaceful and write about his or her response. What do you need to do for the sake of being at peace with yourself and God?

29
The Perils of Communication

Something to Think About

I was in a department store not too long ago. A mother-daughter pair got my attention as the young woman selected a pullover from a pile on a table. She turned to her mother and lifted it up for inspection. Her mother cast a short glare and heaved a huge sigh and raised her eyes to heaven as if pleading for just one more moment of tolerance.

The girl's hand dropped. Neither of them had said a word yet. She shifted her weight to one hip. The corner of her mouth, darkened with an almost black lipstick, curled up.

"No," said the mother softly.

"I like it," the girl said with force.

"You like that hair too. If you didn't wear it that way you wouldn't like the shirt."

The girl spun on the heel of her combat boot and dived back into the pile of shirts on the table. Her mother had been turned away from, ignored, one too many times. She had found her voice.

Right there in Fashion Bug.

She grabbed the girl's shoulders and spun her around. You could tell by the horrified look on the teenager's face that her mother was not given to diatribes among the T-shirts and sweats in department stores. I don't think it had ever occurred to her that Mom had a breaking point that she might reach in Fashion Bug some Tuesday afternoon.

She held her daughter's shoulders in trembling hands. With fire in her pale eyes she told the girl how much she hated her "damn haircut" and that she stayed up nights waiting for the sound of her to come home and that one night last week she walked the streets around the house wishing for just a sight of her and had left the porch light on and ". . . you didn't think about me while you were out there, did you? You didn't think about how worried I would be. You never do. I am the one person you can always turn to. I am the one who will never stop loving you and you walk away from me and you turn to those creepy friends of yours and you lock me out. . . ."

Communicate with someone you live with, someone you have something to say to, someone who will still care what you have to say in twenty years.

A quiet hatred took over the girl's face. She could not believe her mother would do this to her in Fashion Bug. She would not ever forget it. Forgive her? Not a chance. The mask of cold rage closed tight on her pretty young face.

Making It Mine

We are hiding behind technology these days. We talk to strangers on the Internet and ignore the people in our own homes. Kids' rooms look like launch command centers. They are hooked up to communicate with the universe while their families quietly seethe and come apart.

To disconnect from the madness takes a decision, not a decision against anything. But a decision in favor of something — communication. There is no innate evil in today's marvels of communication. I enjoy it as much as the next person. The problem isn't the technology. We're the problem, you and me and our tired minds that are ever seeking the easy way.

I think we'll witness an escalation of Fashion Bug incidents. Public places offer a certain kind of security because there are boundaries for behavior. The mother needed that security. It probably kept her from doing bodily damage to the black-lipped chop-haired little darling who lives in her house.

There was no music, no computer, no fax machine, no beeper, no television, and no bedroom door for the girl to slam shut. She couldn't get away from her mother's desperate act of love. A confusing act of love. One I hope they can each someday forgive.

Now, here's my bold suggestion — let's use the gadgets we own to talk to someone we love, or drop a note to someone who has touched the lines of our face, or sat in the dark with us. Communicate with someone you live with, someone you have something to say to, someone who will still care what you have to say in twenty years.

Prayer Starter

Whoever is wise, let him heed these things
and consider the great love of the Lord.

Psalm 107:43

God, it's just easier not to communicate sometimes. I don't like being hassled, and talking to some people feels like I'm setting myself up to be hassled. I will try though. You have given me people who care about me and so I will try.

Soul Writing

What do you think is the attraction of the Internet, chat rooms, e-mail, etc.? How could you use the technology to really communicate with the people closest to you? Write a letter to someone in your family telling them how you feel.

30
Haunted by Christ

Something to Think About

In the movie *Nell*, Jodie Foster plays the central character, a woman who grows up in the forest alone after her mother dies. She knows nothing of the world beyond her woods and nothing of things like electricity, television, movies, politics, sports, entertainment, trends and fashions, etc. She is discovered though, studied, and then well-meaning folks decide that it is in her best interest to join the rest of human society so that she can lead a "normal" life. In the end her fate is in the hands of a twelve-person jury. She speaks to them in the primal language she knows and is translated by a woman who has studied her.

She says: "You have big things. You know big things. But you don't look into each other's eyes. And, you're hungry for quiet."

The jury begins to realize that she is not going to defend herself; instead, she is going to tell them the truth about themselves.

"I've lived a small life," she says, "and I know only small things." She turns to face the judge. "But the quiet forest is full of angels. In the daytime there comes beauty; in the nighttime, there comes happiness. Don't be afraid for Nell. Don't weep for Nell. I have no greater sorrows than yours."

Nell was mostly unacquainted with sorrow until she took on the sorrow of the human race. Her acquaintance with sorrow is that of experiencing another's pain, loss, lacking, sorrow. This is how Nell is like Christ.

No matter how much we know, or how self-sufficient we become, some part of us remembers that we need a Savior.

Making It Mine

Pay close attention and you'll notice that Hollywood is haunted by Christ. Many, many movies contain a Christ-figure. Someone who brings good news to everyone else, who changes people's lives, who gives him- or herself completely for everyone else.

This is true of older movies like *Cool Hand Luke* (starring

Paul Newman) and newer movies like *The Green Mile* (based on Stephen King's six-part novel by that title) or the popular sci-fi hit *The Matrix*.

The general order of Western civilization is based on a Christian worldview. This reality permeates literature, music, and all the arts, including filmmaking. It isn't always easy to spot the haunting Christ anymore. But he's still there. He shows up in rock songs about being a stranger on a bus and in television shows where angels talk abut God's love. Why do we still find him between the lines and in all the empty places?

Maybe because we know, as St. Teresa wrote, that "Christ has no body now on earth but ours; no hands but ours; no feet but ours." Maybe because no matter how much we know, or how self-sufficient we become, some part of us remembers that we need a Savior.

 # Prayer Starter

Where can I go from your Spirit?
Where can I flee from your presence?
If I go up to the heavens, you are there;
if I make my bed in the depths,
you are there.
If I rise on the wings of the dawn,
if I settle on the far side of the sea,
even there your hand will guide me,
your right hand will hold me fast.

Psalm 139:7-10

Christ has no body now on earth but ours;
no hands but ours;
no feet but ours.
Ours are the eyes
through which Christ's compassion
is to look upon the world.
Ours are the feet
with which he is to go about doing good.
Ours are the hands
with which he is to bless others now.

St. Teresa of Ávila

Soul Writing

Write about a movie you have seen that is "Christ-haunted." What is the importance of the Christ-figure for you and how does this person change the lives of others in the movie? How can Christ change your life?

31
Without Words

Something to Think About

Here's a scene from one daytime drama: A young man has been shot in the throat and for months he cannot talk. After a lot of work and a great deal of soul-searching he says to the friend who has helped him speak again that his inability to talk taught him to communicate without words. It taught him to give his heart to others and allow them to come close enough so that they could sense what he feels without being told. He said, "I learned that silence communicates in ways words never can."

We fill the silence up with background noise or empty chatter rather than enter the silence bravely and see what happens.

In an interview not too long ago, music legend Billy Joel talked about the moment when he was saying good-bye to his daughter and he experienced something that could not be expressed in words. But he found music for the emotion, music without words. He said that he's now writing music without words because it has the ability to say things that can't be said in words.

You might have a friend like one of mine. His words are direct and uncomplicated. But between the lines and in the silences, he jams meaning. He doesn't do it to hide anything; he isn't trying to be mysterious. He isn't playing games. He's just too real for words to express the depths of his spirit and soul. It takes something more. It takes silence.

Making It Mine

For about a year I worked as a facilitator for a support group. This is how we worked. At the beginning of every meeting I would talk a little about the topic of the evening (this was taken from a workbook everyone was supposed to be working on at home during the rest of the week) and I would usually discuss my own experience with the subject.

Typically, the topics were tough ones: forgiveness, telling the truth, admitting to the pain that we hide from others, etc. After I talked a few minutes, it was up to everyone else to join in. No one had to speak — that was understood. However, it was also understood that to get the most from these times together, participation was needed.

It was not usually a problem getting these eight or ten people to talk. But every once in a while I would finish talking and we would just sit there, silent and waiting. The first time this happened, I experienced intense anxiety and had to push down the urge to rush in and fill the silence. Silence, I have learned, is not something that should be ended. Silence is often doing some work in someone; it is accomplishing something, and the most productive thing to do is to stay with the process.

I think we're addicted to words, or at least, noise. We fill the silence up with background noise or empty chatter rather than enter the silence bravely and see what happens.

 ## Prayer Starter

Be still, and know that I am God.

Psalm 46:10a

Lord, I want to silently be with you, to shut my eyes, relax my body, and be still. Why would this sound so frightening at times and so like heaven at other times? Here I am, willing to meet you without all the words and trusting that you'll show up.

Soul Writing

Spend two hours alone in silence without any words at all. I'd like to stretch the reader a little — an hour hardly does that. Write about your feelings and what it was like. Talk to someone you trust about the experience.

32
Really Loving

Something to Think About

I hold this to be the highest task of a bond between two people: that each one should stand guard over the solitude of the other. . . . They are to encourage each other's solitude and their times together are true sharings which interrupt periods of deep isolation. . . . Once the awareness is granted, that even between the closest of human beings there remains an infinite distance, then a wonderful living-alongside-each-other can spring up.

Rainer Rilke

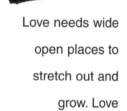

Love needs wide open places to stretch out and grow. Love needs time.

Let there be spaces in your togetherness and let the winds of heaven dance between you. . . . Sing and dance together and be joyous, but let each of you be alone.

Kahlil Gibran

Sometimes you have to let the wind blow through you and me and everything in between.

Charlie Peacock

Making It Mine

"Learn to be still," advises former Eagles' band member Don Henley in the song of the same title. But getting still inside means being alone outside. And that is what prevents us from becoming quiet inside.

"You'd do anything to silence all the voices in your head. . . . Learn to be still."

Loving other people and loving ourselves doesn't really happen unless we can become enough at ease with ourselves to be alone and to be quiet. The poets and musicians quoted here have something very similar in mind. Loving someone, really loving that person, doesn't mean crowding that individual or allowing him or her to smother us either. Real love gives space; it steps back; it doesn't mob us, gang up on us, or hold on to us too tightly. Loving others and loving ourselves requires that we encourage the ones we love in their solitude and independence and that we give the same to ourselves.

The portrait of love often painted in music, movies, television, and books is that of jealous, possessive love — a love that can't stand to have the object of its affection out of its sight for even a moment. That, however, isn't love; it's simply average petty obsession. Selfishness. Immaturity. It's cheaper than love — pretty common really and not at all remarkable.

Learn to hold lightly and enjoy the spaces between. Love needs wide open places to stretch out and grow. Love needs time.

Prayer Starter

The Lord is good to all;
he has compassion on all he has made.
The Lord is righteous in all his ways
and loving toward all he has made.

Psalm 145:9, 17

Love is patient, love is kind. It does not envy, it does not boast, it is not proud. It is not rude, it is not self-seeking, it is not easily angered, it keeps no record of wrongs. Love does not delight in evil but rejoices with the truth. It always protects, always trusts, always hopes, always perseveres.

Love never fails. . . .

1 Corinthians 13:4-8

God, before I call it loving or not loving, before I toss a label at it, remind me to look deeper, think harder, and consider carefully the holy places I enter when I speak of loving.

Soul Writing

Write your own definition of what love is and how it behaves. From where or who do you gather your images of what loving means? Think of instances in which you have seen love portrayed in an appropriate and accurate manner in music and movies.

33
Selling Ourselves

Something to Think About

My youngest brother cut his hair. He's in his late twenties. His hair was, at least in my mind, a sign of his determination to carve out his own path. It was a sign of his resistance to conformity. I have no indication that my brother has actually sold out. He assures me he hasn't. But he looks like the cover of *GQ* magazine. For years he's been told he'll get a better job, make more money, if he cuts his hair. He hasn't listened, until now. He told me he cut it because he's going bald anyway.

Every major bookstore has shelves of books about how to sell yourself. Presenting the self in the best light and treating oneself like a commodity is just how the business world works. In our culture it is something we teach our young. In the last few years I have heard parents of children from infancy to the late teens make the following remarks.

"Isn't the purpose of child-rearing to launch a person who will be a productive member of society with marketable skills by which he can live independently and comfortably?"

"I want my daughter to go to college so that she gets a good job and can have anything she wants."

"Children should not remain a part of their parental unit all their lives."

"My children are gorgeous and intelligent — those are assets they can cash in on forever. These traits are the most important things their father and I have given them. But if they don't develop these gifts and learn how to sell themselves, we'll have to remind ourselves that we did our part by giving them the genetics for success. We aren't failures just because they don't use their gifts profitably."

Now, here's a paradox. Never before have we Americans heard so much noise about developing ourselves, personal growth, actualization of the personal self, core values, true paths, and following our bliss. Yet, never before have so many people been so quick to make commodities of themselves and their children in the name of prosperity and success.

What if our lives were places where people could just be together? What if we loved what we do, even when we aren't rich and others don't understand?

 # Making It Mine

By the time Joe was sixteen, he was a loser. Life had passed him over. He dropped out of high school and went to live among the dead. He became a cemetery keeper. It was 1939 and people weren't as sensitive or considerate of those who have mental handicaps. Joe took a lot of abuse, taking it with a grin. They just figured he didn't know any better.

Joe's job was keeping the headstones from toppling and righting the results of vandalism and straightening up things that fall: flags, vases, wreaths. He kept weeds out of the places where others buried their loves and their hurts. He kept vigil in the place where the truth gets us all — death.

He lived in one room on the grounds, in a sandstone building where the equipment he used was also stored. He had a bed and dresser, a table and two chairs, a stove for heating and cooking. He had a crucifix, a drawing made by a child, and a picture of a child in front of a carousel. That's where he stayed most of the time because his trips into town became harder and harder as World War II filled the cemetery and took over the lives of the townspeople. Joe became a reminder of the big awful thing happening in the world and they didn't want to see him anymore. After the war ended, Joe was pretty entrenched in his isolation.

Joe told a friend that all their stories were written on the headstones, so he didn't feel alone. Headstones said things like, "Now I lay me down to sleep," and "A hero sleeps here," and "Good night, my prince." Joe took very good care of those headstones because he considered them "the story of someone's life." He thought about his own story. He thought about the words that would tell his story.

He went to the township board with a request that when he died they not put a marker on his grave, but erect a bench. He had the money, which he'd been saving for years. He said he wanted it to be "a kind of place where people can sit awhile and talk . . . just be together." He had ideas about what to write on the bench as the story of his life. The college intern at the local newspaper was at the meeting.

He talked to the young writer about his ideas. A really young writer who didn't know if she would ever be able to follow her dream because her life was so complicated and scary. He said he wanted "easy" words on the bench. He talked about a game he remembered as a kid.

"They usually made me It," he said. "I never asked to be It, but that's what they made me. But when I wasn't It, I would run hard to get home and then I'd holler, 'Home free!' " Home free, that's what he wanted written on the bench. Home free. He looked into the young writer's eyes, hoping she'd get it. She did.

Our search for who we are will take us into ultimate encounters with ourselves. To cash that search in for a big salary is the cheap way out. There's nothing wrong with money itself. It's what we do for it that kills us.

What if our lives were places where people could just be together? What if we loved what we do, even when we aren't rich and others don't understand? Like Joe. Does that sound like failure to you? What if what we're trading our bliss for isn't much more than thirty pieces of silver?

 # Prayer Starter

I waited patiently for the Lord;
he turned to me and heard my cry.
He lifted me out of the slimy pit,
out of the mud and mire;
he set my feet on a rock
and gave me a firm place to stand.

Psalm 40:1-2

God, lead me on the path of authenticity. It is a narrow road and not an easy path. When I am distracted, remind me that it is important I be true to who I am. Keep me from selling myself.

Soul Writing

Have you given much thought to your bliss? What is the thing you are most passionate about doing with your life? What gifts and talents do you have? How do you enjoy using them? What do you think God wants you to do with your life?

34
To Judge Or Not to Judge

Something to Think About

It was two days after the slaughter at Columbine High School in Littleton, Colorado. I was in a small-town grocery store with my daughter's baby, Gina, who was about a year old. People like Gina; they smile at her wherever she goes. Even back then she tried very hard to make small talk with strangers and would very often rattle off a long string of sounds that sounded exactly like sentences . . . well, sentences in another language, but sentences still. I've often thought of saying to her, "Gina, you'll have to speak English or these nice people won't be able to understand you."

Anyway, she was doing her magic on the woman checking us out. She had engaged her with a warm "Hi!" as her big blue eyes fixed on the woman. For a brief moment many people forget they're looking into the face of a thumb-sucking, bunny-toting, diaper-clad infant. She has the moves and the look. So the woman looked at her, smiled, and said, "Hi sweetheart, are you helping with the shopping?"

Judging. That's one of those things Jesus made no bones about — don't judge, he said, not unless you'd like to be judged.

To which she replied something like, "haggyboivernlogmabyeiyesuhbacklebacklemoe?" and pointed directly to aisle number 3 with this "Can't you see what's going on over there?" tone of voice, deeply furrowed brow, and her head tilted to one side. The clerk looked confused. Gina waited about three seconds for a reply and then said, "huh?youhuh?"

I bailed her out. "She's only eleven months old."

"What a remarkable little girl," the clerk said with relief. "And so cute too."

It was then the guy behind me spoke up. He was an older man, sort of stooped over and tired-looking. "Sure, she's cute now, but then they go and blow up their school! Not so cute then, are they?" He spoke with the resentment of a man who had doubtlessly been warning strangers about the devious nature of children all of his life and now . . . well, now, he had proof. Gina turned her scowl upon him and then popped her thumb in her mouth and leaned forward to tuck her head under my chin and rest against me.

I couldn't resist.

I looked him in the eye and said, "Look what you've done. You've hurt her feelings. Have a nice day!"

He got out of line and went to another cash register.

 ## Making It Mine

None of us would want to be frozen in the worst moment of our lives. In the same way, no group of people wants to be identified by the destructive or negative actions of a few within its group. Stereotypes freeze people in what is negative.

And so all old men become child molesters, all teens become gun-toting, drug-taking gang members, all Southern women become passive Barbie dolls, and all football players become violent morons.

All of us make some kinds of judgments. If we didn't, we would be unable to select who to be friends with, who to fall in love with, who to trust, who to avoid. This process is a good thing and it prevents us from making mistakes that would haunt us for a lifetime. It is a different process than dismissing people by labeling them as X without knowing their story or the truth about them.

It's ironic that teenagers — who are so often stereotyped by the media, education system, entertainment industry, and most of our culture — are among the most guilty of branding others with stereotypes. Whether it's jocks or alternative types or losers, there's a title for everyone in the halls of high school. By trashing people into neat little predictable categories, the process of getting to know others and learning to accept them is bypassed.

Ever heard your friends talking about someone judging them? Have you ever said yourself that you feel judged by others, maybe family, peers, or people who go to church? Stereotyping is judging. Before you can slap someone with a label, a judgment has to be rendered about that person.

Judging. That's one of those things Jesus made no bones about — don't judge, he said, not unless you'd like to be judged. How you treat others, that's how you'll be treated.

Prayer Starter

Do not judge, or you too will be judged. For in the same way you judge others, you will be judged, and with the measure you use, it will be measured to you.

Matthew 7:1

Teach me knowledge and good judgment,
for I believe in your commands.

Psalm 119:66

Holy Judge, it's easy to stereotype people and make judgments without giving it much thought. It happens before I think about what I'm doing. Teach me to stop, think, and resist the impulse to judge. Keep my mind and heart open.

Soul Writing

Pay attention to how often you hear others judging people and write about it. Try to go a full forty-eight hours without judging anyone. Write about what happened and how you felt. How do you feel when others judge you?

35
The Question Is Why

Something to Think About

When I was a medical student, I participated in the interview of a patient admitted to a psychiatric hospital for depression. The patient was a Jew who had survived Hitler's "final solution." His young daughter did not survive, however, and he could not forget the day that decided her fate.

According to him, the Nazi guards paraded the inmates before them to decide who would be chosen for slave labor and who would be used for "medical experimentation." This man walked hand in hand with his daughter as they approached one of the guards.

Don't stand alone clutching your doubts silently. Talk to someone you trust.

The guard indicated that the father should join the labor force to the left, but his daughter should go with the group to the right. As they understood the implication, his daughter held to his hand tighter and begged her papa to protect her. The impatient soldier poised his bayonet over their clutched hands in unambiguous threat. As the child grasped her father's hand more tightly, the guard began lowering his bayonet as if to sever their hold on each other. At this, the poor man let go of his daughter's hand. She was led away to the right and to her death. The father survived but was haunted for the rest of his life by the fact that he had let go of her hand. He saw her death as his own fault.

Adapted from *Children Are Images of Grace:
A Pediatrician's Trilogy of Faith, Hope and Love*
by Diane M. Komp, M.D.

Making It Mine

The suffering of innocents is a problem for anyone who wants to believe in a loving and just God. We must not accept simplistic explanations such as children deserving to suffer, children paying for the sins of others, or children suffering because God has willed it. If any of those things are true, God does not deserve to be God and certainly deserves no love or allegiance from any of us.

The only satisfaction I have found — the only answer I have found — is that God joined himself to the suffering of the innocent in his dying on the cross. That God does not stand at a distance from suffering, but that this suffering is personal and felt and deeply significant to God. Why does God do nothing?

Who knows?

Fyodor Dostoyevsky's character Ivan in *The Brothers Karamazov* says this, "Suffering will be healed and made up for. . . . At the moment of eternal harmony, something so precious will come to pass that it will suffice for all hearts, for the comforting of all resentments, for the atonement of all crimes of humanity of all the blood they've shed; that it will make it not only possible to forgive, but to justify all that has happened with men."

Oddly enough, in the novel Ivan is able to articulate this Christian belief but is unable to accept it, saying that heaven exacts too high a price for this hope.

Flannery O'Connor wrote, "I think there is no suffering greater than what is caused by the doubts of those who want to believe. I know what torment this is, but I can only see it, in myself anyway, as the process by which faith is deepened. . . . What people don't realize is how much religion costs. They think faith is a big electric blanket, when of course it is a cross. It is much harder to believe than not to believe. If you feel you can't believe, you must at least do this: keep an open mind. Keep it open toward faith, keep wanting it, keep asking for it, and leave the rest to God. . . ."

Doubt that is born in your desire to believe is nothing to be afraid of. It is the healthy sign of a maturing spirituality and an honest approach to life. Don't stand alone clutching your doubts silently. Talk to someone you trust. But as O'Connor writes, "Don't expect faith to clear things up for you. [Faith] is trust, not certainty."

Prayer Starter

Show me your ways, O Lord,
teach me your paths;
guide me in your truth and teach me,
for you are God my Savior,
and my hope is in you all day long.

Psalm 25:4-5

Lord, I need realistic expectations of myself and my faith. When I wrestle with doubts please reassure me that you understand. Help me not to search for answers but for hope.

Soul Writing

When was the last time you asked God, "Why?" Write about the thing that prompted your question. Has the question been resolved or are you still struggling with the issue? Is there someone you can talk with about it? What positive thing can you do to help yourself handle doubts?

36
Living with a Conscience

Something to Think About

The author Bill Bryson and his companion are attempting to hike the Appalachian Trail. They were joined on the journey by a young but obnoxious woman who was alone. This scene happens shortly after they ditch her in the woods.

You are responsible to know what is right and wrong to act accordingly.

Even as I said these things, I realized with a kind or horrible weeping awareness that he was right. We had ditched her, left her to the bears and wolves and chortling mountain men. I had been so completely preoccupied with my own savage lust for food and a real bed that I had not paused to consider what our abrupt departure would mean for her: a night alone among the whispering trees, swaddled in darkness, listening with involuntary keenness for the telltale crack of a branch or stick under a heavy foot or paw. It wasn't something I would wish on anyone. My gaze fell on my pie, and I realized I didn't want it any longer. "Maybe she'll have found someone to camp with," I suggested lamely, and pushed the pie away.

"Did you see anybody today?"

He was right. We had seen hardly a soul.

"She's probably still walking right now," Katz said with a hint of sudden heat. "Wondering where the hell we got to. Scared out of her chubby little wits."

"Oh, don't," I half pleaded, and distractedly pushed the pie a half inch farther away.

He nodded an empathetic, busy, righteous little nod, and looked at me with a strange, glowing, accusatory expression that said, "And if she dies, let it be on your conscience." And he was right; I was the ringleader here. This was my fault.

From *A Walk in the Woods* by Bill Bryson

Making It Mine

Guilt is getting a bad name these days. Pick up a self-help book and you'll read about how negative guilt is, how useless it is. Catholics are stereotyped as guilt-infested neurotics. Hardly anyone stands up and admits that sometimes we do things for which we rightly feel guilt — if our conscience is properly formed.

There are two kinds of guilt. There's the kind of guilt that is indeed very bad for you. This is when you feel guilt for what you clearly have no responsibility. If you've been sexually assaulted, it isn't your fault, not ever. If your parent is an alcoholic, it's not your fault. If your parents divorce, your sister flunks fourth grade, or there is war in China, it is not your fault. Guilt, though common in some of these instances, is destructive and unhealthy. This is the kind of guilt that gets into your gut and rots you from the inside out. If you carry this kind of guilt around, you'll never be a happy, whole person until you dump the guilt.

The other kind of guilt is rightful guilt. It is what happens when we do something wrong. Steal. Cheat. Betray. Lie. If you mistreat someone without feeling guilt you've got a pretty serious problem. The absence of this kind of guilt shows up in people like serial killers and lifelong criminals. Guilt is uncomfortable, but it is not unhealthy. Genuine guilt moves you to purge yourself of whatever is tying you up in knots and to make amends for your actions.

In the sacrament of reconciliation Catholics have a chance to get rid of guilt completely and start over again. It's not an easy fix. Madonna said once that she knew she could sin on Tuesday and go to confession on Saturday and be right with God. That's not what confession is for and no one believes that line of bull. It's easy criticism from people who don't want to do the tough thing and peer into the dark places inside.

There's dignity in this. You aren't a robot; you don't have anyone else making choices for you. You are expected to figure this moral stuff out and to take it seriously. Catholics regard conscience as God's gift to us. The *Catechism of the Catholic Church* puts it this way: "Man [meaning everyone, not just males] has the right to act in conscience and in freedom so as personally to make moral decisions" (No. 1782). You are responsible to know what is right and wrong to act accordingly.

Prayer Starter

Have mercy on me, O God,
according to your unfailing love;
according to your great compassion
blot out my transgressions.
Wash away all my iniquity
and cleanse me from my sin.

Psalm 51:1-2

Blessed is he
whose transgressions are forgiven,
whose sins are covered.
Blessed is the man
whose sin the Lord does not count against him
and in whose spirit is no deceit.
I said, "I will confess my transgressions to the Lord" —
and you forgave
the guilt of my sin.

Psalm 32:1-2, 5b

Father, I am thankful that you don't deal with us according to our sins, but instead remove them from us at such distances I can't imagine. Create in me a brand-new heart, a true heart, from the ashes of my burned-up and broken one. Help me to stay close to you and stop all this sinning.

Soul Writing

Describe your experience with both kinds of guilt. How do you feel about each kind? When did you last confess your sins? How did you feel afterward? Make a list of what you would like to confess in the sacrament of reconciliation.

37
Better Than You Know

Something to Think About

The author is head of the volunteer fire department in this small town in northern Minnesota. One night at 10:30 he gets a call that the Pine Beach Resort is burning. Despite the firefighters' best efforts, the resort is a total loss.

There is something embedded in the human spirit, something substantial with God's presence, that rises up and meets the challenge of hard times.

The owners' reaction was painful to watch. A horrified exclamation, a scream of anguish, a collapse into the arms of friends and relatives. But we were relieved to learn that one of the men we feared lost in the blaze had returned with the owners. And he assured us that the other man, too, was safe, as the building had been empty after all. That made the night, and prospect of morning, a lot less dreary.

As the night wore on, the owners became at least a little reconciled to the devastating spectacle before them, and they began to exhibit behavior I've seen time and again, but still find surprising. In the midst of their loss, when you'd expect them to be too dejected to respond, they can't stop heaping affection on the firefighters. Here is a person's house, business, or whatever more than likely gutted or lying in smoking ruins, and there they are, thanking, congratulating, and praising us. In most cases we haven't even saved the place, and still people laud our efforts and often promise monetary donations to the department, promises that're invariably kept. I'm always a bit embarrassed.

You wish you could have done more, and sometimes blame yourself for variables of time and distance that were beyond your control. To the owners, though, you appear as angels of mercy. You responded to their call for help, and they can see that you tried your best. They are deeply moved that fellow members of their community came running through the winter night or pouring rain, setting aside their own concerns or leaving a warm bed, and put their health and safety on the line. It injects a note of hope and camaraderie into an otherwise dismal situation and goes a long way toward helping people through the crisis of personal loss.

From *Letters from Side Lake: A Chronicle of Life in the North Woods* by Peter M. Leschak

 # Making It Mine

Not long ago I was traveling to Chicago and was stranded at the airport for a while. When I arrived, there were a number of people who had been stranded a very long time. I expected the situation to be tense and not very pleasant.

I was wrong. Over the next few hours I watched these people make the best of the situation. People helped others with their children, watched their bags, bought food and shared it. They told jokes, some did magic tricks, and one man even suggested we all fly to Las Vegas. "After all," he joked, "you couldn't be any less lucky than you are right now."

People were frustrated, but no one was barking at the others. The place virtually oozed with consideration, good attitudes, and a hardy sense of humor.

When an airline representative came over to our gate to tell us that planes were going to be able to get in and get us on our way he looked very nervous. When we started to cheer, relief spread over his face and he laughed right out loud with us. I don't know who started it, but I'm convinced that the reason our little band of travelers had managed such great attitudes was probably one traveler with one good attitude.

The longer you live, the more you'll hear stories of how human beings become their very best when they are in difficult situations. There is something embedded in the human spirit, something substantial with God's presence, that rises up and meets the challenge of hard times.

You might wonder if you have it. You do. You don't have any need for it until that moment happens and you have to reach deep inside and show what you're made of. When it happens, you're going to be wonderfully surprised.

Prayer Starter

God is within her, she will not fall;
God will help her at break of day.

Psalm 46:5

You are my hiding place;
you will protect me from trouble
and surround me with songs of deliverance.

Psalm 32:7

Lord, let your kingdom come so that no one hurts or suffers any longer. Let your kingdom come so that the ways of selfishness are abolished. Let your kingdom come to me, inside of me. Make me stronger and better than I know.

Soul Writing

Write about an incident in which you saw how others responded in a time of crisis. Put yourself in that crisis and imagine how you would respond. What makes it possible for us to be so unselfish during difficult times?

38
What's Real, What's Not?

Something to Think About

A few months ago I visited a monastery where Benedictine nuns are taking care of a hundred or so other Benedictine nuns who, after giving their lives to God and others, count on the love of their sisters in their last years. You might think it would be gloomy place, but it wasn't.

I was having breakfast with my traveling companions and a couple of the nuns who run the place. Behind us was a table of very old women who had hauled themselves in there early in the morning, dressed neatly and smiling at one another.

One of the sisters said, "I don't think I'll ever get used to this place. I miss the real world."

Across from her a thin woman dressed in her nun's habit said, "Ha! The real world, have you ever seen such a thing as the real world? Who knows what real is? All I know is that I haven't seen it yet and I'm counting on getting there eventually. " Then she finished her oatmeal with gusto.

Finally a woman so tiny she looked like she would slide beneath the table, pointing her spoon at the three others at her table, said, "I've seen real; I see it all the time, and so do you. It's just hard to talk about."

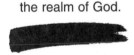

The most real things in your world are what you can't see: love, friendship, justice, dreams, faith. These aren't tangible material things — they are mystery. Mystery is the realm of God.

Making It Mine

What's real? An interesting question. In a relatively recent smash movie, *The Matrix*, two worlds exist side by side. There is the world that everyone sees, one in which all the people who are surely convinced they understand reality go about their daily lives in the sphere of reality. However, it is far from real. The same theme is in the movie *The Truman Show*, starring Jim Carrey. One man's life is carried out on television for all the world to see, but he doesn't know it. An alter reality has been created for him and for all of his life he has accepted it.

It is often what we don't see that makes all the difference. The most real things in your world are what you can't see:

love, friendship, justice, dreams, faith. These aren't tangible material things — they are mystery. Mystery is the realm of God.

Several years ago my family was struggling. It was one of the hardest periods of our lives, and I felt as if I could hardly face another day. Early one morning I was suddenly awake and the bedroom was filled with the smell of Aqua Velva (my father's favorite after-shave lotion; he's been dead many years). Out of nowhere my father's presence seemed to wrap me up and these words were pressed into my heart: "You are never alone. There is always hope. Never stop trying; promise me you'll never stop trying."

That encounter is not real to anyone else. But it is profoundly real to me. And it is one of the most precious moments of my life. If you haven't had that kind of experience, chances are, you will at some point in your life.

Be careful that you don't base your life on what you see. You'll be missing out on the best this universe has to offer.

 # Prayer Starter

So we fix our eyes not on what is seen, but on what is unseen. For what is seen is temporary, but what is unseen is eternal.

2 Corinthians 4:18

But my eyes are fixed on you,
O Sovereign Lord;
in your I take refuge. . . .

Psalm 141:8a

Lord, turn my head toward you every day. Open my eyes to your reality and the joy of spending my life with you in a world filled with surprise at every turn and wonder in every molecule. Be my vision.

 Soul Writing

How do you feel about believing what you can't see? Write about a time when you believed something that seemed obvious but wasn't what it seemed. How would trying to "see" the world as God sees it make a difference in your life?

39
Good Advice

Something to Think About

Go placidly amid the noise and haste, and remember what peace there may be in silence. As far as possible, without surrender, be on good terms with all persons. Speak your truth quietly and clearly; and listen to others, even the dull and ignorant; they too have their story.

Avoid loud and aggressive persons; they are vexatious to the spirit. If you compare yourself with others, you may become bitter or vain, for always there will be greater and lesser persons than yourself. Enjoy your achievements as well as your plans.

Keep interested in your own career, however humble; it is a real possession in the changing fortunes of time. Exercise caution in your business affairs; for the world if full of trickery. But let this not blind you to what virtue there is; many persons strive for high ideals; and everywhere life is full of heroism.

Be yourself. Especially, do not feign affection. Neither be cynical about love; for in the face of all aridity and disenchantment it is perennial as the grass.

Take kindly the counsel of the years, gracefully surrendering the things of youth. Nurture strength of spirit to shield you in sudden misfortune. But do not distress yourself with imaginings. Many fears are born of fatigue and loneliness. Beyond a wholesome discipline, be gentle with yourself.

You are a child of the universe, no less than the trees and the stars; you have a right to be here. And whether or not it is clear to you, no doubt the universe is unfolding as it should.

Therefore be at peace with God, whatever you conceive Him to be, and whatever your labors and aspirations, in the noisy confusion of life keep peace with your soul.

With all its sham, drudgery, and broken dreams, it is still a beautiful world. Be cheerful. Strive to be happy.

Max Ehrmann

All of your life you'll hear advice. You'll hear it from friends, family, teachers. . . . Some of it will make sense to you and seem very true. You'll know.

Making It Mine

Recently a song offering advice to young people climbed to the top of the charts. The writer of the song stated that the only advice he could give for sure was to wear sunblock. Which is good advice. However, the song had other good advice too. And a lot of it isn't anything new.

Laugh hard every day.

Be careful not to buy into the lies the culture and media tell you about yourself.

Stay in touch with people who love you.

Don't give up your dreams.

The one piece of advice that is common to all these creeds, you'll find, is summed up in this line: you have a right to be here. You are an idea of God's. You are not an accident. You are not a splash in the gene pool. Whatever your life is for, no one else's life is for the same thing. If the world misses out on you, it will miss out on what will never be repeated. The universe was created for you.

All of your life you'll hear advice. You'll hear it from friends, family, teachers; you'll hear it in songs and you'll watch it in movies and you'll read books like this one. Some of it will make sense to you and seem very true. You'll know. But when you can't remember any of it because the night has been too long and the world too cold, remember this: you have a right to be here.

Prayer Starter

Praise the Lord, O my soul;
all my inmost being, praise his holy name.
Praise the Lord, O my soul,
and forget not all his benefits —
who forgives all your sins
and heals all your diseases,
who redeems your life from the pit,
and crowns you with love and compassion,
who satisfies your desires with good things,
so that your youth is renewed like the eagle's.

Psalm 103:1-5

Father, the best of me doesn't seem to be enough sometimes. I look for a place that feels right and a thing to do that seems to be what I'm made to do. I have moments when it all makes sense and then the doubts jump on me again. I'm told that you love me regardless of my doubts. There are so many voices that offer advice. Teach me to hear you in the voices. Hang on to me when I struggle and stay with me no matter how dark it gets.

Soul Writing

What is the best advice you've ever been given? What kind of advice do you need right now? Who might be able to offer you guidance? What are the dangers of advice? How can you tell when advice is good for you?

40
The Weird Gift of Family

Something to Think About

For all the frustration and weirdness of it, you'll learn the most important lessons of your life in a family.

Rebecca Veeck, the eight-year-old daughter of baseball owner Mike Veeck, is going blind.

However, in keeping with family tradition started by Mike's father, Bill Veeck (who had a wooden leg) they are handling Rebecca's tragedy with laughter.

It didn't start out that way. Mike Veeck was stunned when his little girl got a diagnosis of a horrible disease called retinitis pigmentosa in 1998. He had always been a strict father but decided to relax his standards. "If she didn't want to sit up straight or eat with a fork or be polite, well, who was I to tell someone who was losing her sight what to do?" he says.

Rebecca, however, didn't like this new version of her once-strict father. When he took her out of school so they could have fun, she complained. When he resigned as the Tampa Bay Devil Rays' vice president of sales in marketing to spend more time with her, it touched off a round of publicity about the situation. Rebecca told him angrily, "Thanks, Dad, now my whole class knows I'm going blind!"

Rebecca reminded her father of her grandfather, who had one leg "and that didn't slow him down," she said. Her father still talks to his now-deceased father, Bill Veeck, when he grows frustrated with baseball. She knew that invoking the name of her grandfather would get her father's attention.

So, Rebecca and her father talked about Bill Veeck. About how he would gather neighborhood children in his yard and drive a nail through his leg challenging them to get their fathers to do the same. Bill painted his wooden leg copper each spring and told everyone he would tan his body to match the color by the end of the summer. Mike and Rebecca started laughing again. After that, she had to sit up straight and she had to use her fork and she had to be polite and go to school.

In the tradition set by Bill Veeck, Mike and Rebecca have a family ritual. As her father turns the key to unlock the door to their home, Rebecca inches up close to the door she can't really see very well and sticks her foot out to feel for it. Then, as her father turns the knob, she stumbles through the doorway and into the door; her father then pulls the door back and hits his own face with it and together they tumble onto the floor in a pile of laughter and hugging. This should not be funny.

Neither should the song they sing together. "Ret-in-i-tis" Mike croons in one part of the house, and from another comes a response from Rebecca, "Pig-men-to-sa!" They call it the R.P. song. When she was diagnosed with the illness, also known as tunnel vision, a doctor from Emory University told the family they would need humor to get through this. Sometimes the parents wonder if they are taking her illness seriously enough. But laughter is a family tradition, and the strength they have found in that tradition has helped all of them cope.

Mike Veeck says he talks to his father about the "crazy" way they're handling Rebecca's illness. "And I hear him laughing. I don't know if I'm doing the right thing," he says, "but I'm doing what I know how to do best."

 # Making It Mine

I was a sophomore in high school when I went on my first date. It was November in Michigan, which meant it was hunting season. Johnny was taking me to a football game and dance. I had planned the night carefully.

My father, Andrew Collins, smiled often, but he didn't laugh much — and when he did he split the rafters with it. For all of my childhood he gave me what so many people crave: his unconditional, unwavering love. He wasn't perfect, but he loved me without fail.

Five minutes before Johnny was due to arrive, my father hauled out his shotgun. Then he sat in a rocker so that he would be the first thing Johnny would see when he walked in. Dad began cleaning his gun. I was horrified. I pleaded with Mom to make him stop; she was having a hard time controlling her laughter. That night has become legend in our family stories.

At 7:00 p.m., Johnny arrived. I threw the door open in exasperation and stepped aside. Johnny stood very still, his really large Adam's apple bobbing around nervously. His eyes fell on me and he smiled shyly and then he saw my father.

"I'm leaving now," I announced.

"Be home by midnight," Dad said, not looking up. But I saw him smile. My father was cleaning his gun because he loved me and he wanted this young man who dared to think himself good enough for his daughter to know I was loved, protected, and cherished.

Families can only be described as weird sometimes. The experience of belonging to one and how we love one another is varied and unpredictable and as wild as a storm. But for the majority of us our families are the best of God's gifts to us. Try to believe that about your parents too. For all the frustration and weirdness of it, you'll learn the most important lessons of your life in a family.

Prayer Starter

A father to the fatherless,
defender of widows,
is God in his holy dwelling.
God sets the lonely in families,
he leads forth the prisoners with singing. . . .

Psalm 68:5-6a

Father of us all, you know it isn't easy belonging to a family. Sometimes, it's almost more than I can take. Let me see the love woven through the relationships. Help me to appreciate every member of my family and be grateful for each and every one of them.

Soul Writing

What do you like most about your family? Write about a way your parents have expressed their love for you. What are you doing to nurture a relationship with your parents? Write a prayer thanking God for your parents.

41
I'm Only Human
(Not That There's Anything Wrong with That)

Something to Think About

Baby Suggs is preaching to her slave parishioners.

She did not tell them to clean up their lives or to go and sin no more. She did not tell them they were the blessed of the earth. . . . She told them that the only grace they could have was the grace they could imagine. That if they could not see it, they would not have it.

"Here," she said, "in this place, we flesh; flesh that weeps, laughs; flesh that dances on bare feet in the grass. Love it. Love it hard. Yonder they do not love your flesh. They despise it. They don't love your eyes: they's just as soon pick 'em out. . . . And, O my people, they do not love your hands. Those they only use, tie, bind, chop off and leave empty. Love your hands! Love them. Raise them up and kiss them. Touch others with them, pat them together, stroke them on your face 'cause they don't love that either.

"You got to love it, you! And no, they ain't in love with your mouth. Yonder out there, they will see it broken and break it again. What you say out of it they will not heed. What you scream from it they do not hear. . . . No, they don't love your mouth. You got to love it. This is the flesh I'm talking about here. Flesh that needs to be loved. Feet that need to rest and dance; backs that need support; . . . And, O my people, out yonder, hear me, they do not love your neck unnoosed and straight. So love your neck; put a hand on it, grace it, stroke it and hold it up."

From *Beloved* by Toni Morrison

Let's say it once and for all: it is a glorious and holy thing to be human. We are capable of great things because we're human.

Making It Mine

"Flesh" as a religious word isn't used much anymore, but when it was, it usually referred to the part of a human that acted upon his or her most animalistic compulsions. "Sins of the flesh" they were called, meaning we were acting not on a divine impulse, but an animalistic one. This often meant a

156

human impulse and confused the two. The message was clear: Being human is your problem. If you can escape your humanness, you can escape the base impulses.

So we hear all sorts of excuses that end in ". . . but I'm only human."

Let's say it once and for all: it is a glorious and holy thing to be human. We are capable of great things because we're human. Rather than using it as an excuse, why not pull ourselves up to our full human potential and when we do something loving, kind, and gracious, say, "Well, of course . . . I am human after all."

In his book *Miracles of the Saints*, author Bert Ghezzi tells the story of St. Teresa of Ávila who lived during a time when holy women and men often indulged in body-punishing ascetical practices. A visitor once found Teresa indulging with delight and relish in the eating of a partridge. The person was shocked by such "fleshly" behavior.

Between bites this wonderfully human saint spouted, "Let them think as they please. There's a time for partridge and a time for penance."

Here in this place, as Baby Suggs tells us, "we flesh." That's how God made it. Just as a frog is its holiest by being a frog and nothing else, we are holiest when we are what we are: "gloriously human." "Love it. Love it hard."

Prayer Starter

Lord, you have searched me out and known me;
You know my sitting and my rising up;
you discern my thoughts from afar.
You trace my journeys and my resting places
and are acquainted with all my ways.
For you yourself created my inmost parts;
you knit me together in my mother's womb.
I will thank you because I am marvelously made;
your works are wonderful, and I know it well.

Psalm 139:1-2, 12-14

Jesus, I know well that there is more to me and more to others than I know. When I seem to be my own worst enemy, please be my best friend. When I forget what a miracle I am, remind me. If I fail to honor others, provoke me to better ways. It is a glorious thing to be human and be who I am because you made me.

Soul Writing

Sometimes circumstances place us where others aren't very good at loving us. People fail. They even try to make us feel bad about ourselves and place blame in all the wrong places. How can you love yourself when others fail to? What do you believe about the goodness (or not) of being human? What are some of the most lovable things about you? What did God create in you that makes you distinctly you?

42
Star Thrower

Something to Think About

Loren Eisely was a scientist on vacation, scouring and roaming and enjoying the shores of Costabel. One early morning he was walking slowly, looking at what the ocean had left on the sandy beach during the night. "In the end," he thought to himself, "the sea rejects its offspring."

He saw star shells with tiny animals still barely alive inside, hundreds of them left by a stormy night on an abandoned shoreline.

It was not dawn yet and he watched in the darkness as professional shell collectors gathered bags full of dying starfish. The human figures seemed like greedy scavengers to him, preying upon the abandoned and dying stars.

He walked around a bluff, and the rising sun projecting light into the still stormy sky dropped a giant rainbow over the beach and there at the end of the rainbow was another human figure, circled with color, stooping over, picking up stars, and flinging them back into the surf. Again and again, he stooped and picked up and flung the still-living things back into the sea.

"It's still alive," Eisely commented to the man.

He nodded. "Yes, it may live if the offshore pull is strong enough," he said gently. The scientist walked on, at one point he turned and watched the star thrower for a moment.

Later, in his famous essay "The Star Thrower," he wrote: ". . . he appeared magnified, as though casting larger stars upon some greater sea. . . ." But Eisely thought again and blinked and reordered his reality and thought, "No, he is a man . . . the star thrower is a man, and on every beach in the world death is running with more speed than this single star thrower."

He thought of Darwin, who said that death is the sad but realistic rule of progress; he pondered Freud and the inner struggle of light and darkness in the human soul. He thought of tornadoes and twisters and he remembered a picture of his mother as a child, so young, so very young and already with a

From your mother's womb to the waters of baptism you are cast into the ocean of God's love and your life is claimed by the One who gave it to you to start with.

haunted look in her eyes. He remembered the biblical quote ". . . Love not the world, neither the things that are in the world"; and then he thought, "But I do love the world. I love the small ones, the things beaten in the strangling surf; I love the lost ones; I love the failures." And he thought, "I have to go back and help the star thrower."

He walked back to stand near the man; he picked up a star and he threw it as far as he could fling it and he picked one up again and threw and threw and threw. He was hurling life back into life like a madman who believed in life in some way that he had only discovered that morning on the edge of dawn. He said that as he flung, he felt that he and the star thrower were standing beside "an unknown Hurler of suns" casting stars on some eternal beach.

From "The Star Thrower" by Loren Eiseley,
in *The Star Thrower*

Making It Mine

The Spinner of the Universe sent into our world a Star Thrower. His name was Jesus; he lived in a little town, born to a working-class family in a country under military occupation. Our record of his life is somewhat sketchy, and people disagree over some of the details, but this much is undisputed: he spent his life throwing dying stars into the ocean of God where they would come alive again. He came to us and said, "I love the world. I love the misfits and the forgotten; I love the little ones and the lost ones; I love the weary ones. I love every single lost human star washed onto the shore of life and taking its final breath."

He went about commanding that people live. To the one dying, he said, "Live!" To the proud and young and rich he said, "Live!" He met the eyes of the fisherman, the prostitute, the tax collector, the rabbi, and with the fire of God burning in the night he whispered soul to soul, "Live!"

For three short years he was a single soul sowing life in the fields of death. He came to this small beach and he found the children of God, stars of God, dying on the shores, and he threw them back to their Originator that they might live. He comes to us in our sickness, in our hopelessness. He comes to tired young mothers and weary old men. He comes to teenagers who think they can't get out of bed one more morning. He comes to the proud who think they have all the answers, and in the ghetto of our selfishness, in the boredom of our youth, he says, "Live!"

He picks us up and hurls us into the ocean of God's love and we live. From your mother's womb to the waters of baptism you are cast into the ocean of God's love and your life is claimed by the One who gave it to you to start with. Then he comes to you and me and he puts a star in our hands and he says, "This is what you were born for: throw the star." You star of God, salvaged from the shores of death, you are a star thrower too.

Prayer Starter

The Lord's right hand has done mighty things!
The Lord's right hand is lifted high;
the Lord's right hand has done mighty things!

Psalm 118:15b-16

I want to join you in saving my world. Help me see myself as a star thrower. Infuse me with faith to believe it is true.

Soul Writing

Write about the differences between the star thrower and the people on the beach who were collecting the stars. Which kind of person are you? What do you believe you were born to do?

43
How Dare You Love Yourself?

Something to Think About

Chris DeVinck was hungry for an English muffin. His kids were outside playing. He pulled out the toaster.

After a few moments the muffins popped up and were ready for butter. . . . The back door crashed open. "Mmmmmm! Muffins!" Karen called out. "Can I have one?"

Caught in my solitude.

"Sure. I have to get one out of the freezer."

As I pulled the chrome handle of the refrigerator, Karen skipped past me. The coolness circled my hand with that familiar mist; I reached into the freezer. I was trying to pull a muffin out of the bag when I heard a loud scream. I turned to see Karen curled up on the kitchen floor sobbing.

"Ow! Ow! It hurts. Daddy, it hurts so much."

I quickly knelt on the floor and embraced Karen.

"Karen, what happened?" I asked between her weeping. All she managed to do was hold her mouth and weep.

Karen had kissed the toaster, the still-burning toaster. As she came bouncing into the kitchen after her performance on her bicycle, she saw her reflection in the toaster and she kissed her own image. . . .

From *Only the Heart Knows How to Find Them*
by Christopher DeVinck

Our struggle in life is to make a mark and make a difference.

Making It Mine

It's a cliché: You can't love anyone else until you learn to love yourself. But cliché or otherwise, it's not an easy thing to do. Culture, religious beliefs, the things others say about us — these get in the way of loving self. In a culture like ours, trying to love yourself can sting as much as kissing a hot toaster.

A while back, my family visited an abandoned lighthouse on the shores of Lake Superior. We took the stairs — a harder climb, but it gave us time to talk, see the view on every level, and read the messages left behind by other pilgrims. Scrawled messages were everywhere on the walls: "Judy lived and loved."

"I've been here." "When is it my turn?" "Mike and LuAnn Married 1988." "John was here."

We write such things because we have a deep-down sense of our worth. The other graffiti, the ugly kind, comes from a fear of dying without letting anyone ever see the ugly side of ourselves. At least that's what one college professor of mine suggested.

Life is a lot like the climb to the top of the lighthouse. Twisting, breathless, dark in places, light in places, and sometimes it opens up to unexpected beauty. At the end, after the journey . . . well, you can't even begin to imagine what the view is going to be like, way up at the top of it all.

Along the way, we discover ourselves; we learn to love ourselves even though it will be painful sometimes and we leave our marks. Everyone isn't going to understand. There will be times when loving yourself will come hard and you'll have to remind yourself that you are worth it, that there's something good in you. That is the ultimate reality about you. You are good and you are worth loving.

Our struggle in life is to make a mark and make a difference. We don't want to build a monument to ourselves. It's good to believe you're good. If you have trouble believing that, remember that God declared our goodness on the first day. We are marked with goodness. It might take all your lifetime and an exhausting, exhilarating climb toward heaven before that goodness is fully realized — just keep climbing.

Prayer Starter

For you created my inmost being;
you knit me together in my mother's womb.
I praise you because I am fearfully and wonderfully made;
your works are wonderful,
I know that full well.
My frame was not hidden from you
when I was made in the secret place.
When I was woven together in the depths of the earth.

Psalm 139:13-15

Father, I am a mixed bag. I hold it all up to you. My strength, my wonder, my mystery, my wounds, my sinfulness. I often have no sense of who I am or what I might become. Take me onward into a truer, deeper love for myself and for others. Let me always be honest with myself.

Soul Writing

What comes to mind when you think about loving yourself? What do you think it means to love yourself? Is it easy or difficult for you to love yourself? Write about this.

44
Can It Be Beautiful Because It's Broken?

Something to Think About

In the classic tale The Secret Garden *(now a movie), Colin who has long believed himself unable to walk and ready to die has been healed by long days of friendship in the secret garden and by some Magic he never knew existed. In this passage he finally tells someone about it.*

The healing touch will find you, will find all of us. Don't ever stop believing it.

It was because she seemed such a wonderful woman in her nice moorland way that at last she was told about the Magic.

"Do you believe in Magic?" asked Colin. ". . . I do hope that you do."

"That I do, lad," she answered. "I never knowed it by that name, but what does the name matter? I warrant they call it a different name in France and a different one in Germany. The same thing as sets the seeds swellin' and the sun shinin' made thee a well lad and it's the Good Thing. . . . The Big Good Thing doesn't stop to worry, . . . It goes on makin' worlds by the million. . . . Never thee stop believin' in the Big Good Thing and knowin' the world's full of it. . . ."

From *The Secret Garden* by Frances Hodgson Burnett

Making It Mine

Visitors to the royal palace in Tehran, Iran, report that it's stunningly beautiful. Stepping into the palace you're surrounded with millions of fragments of gleaming, sparkling light. The domed ceiling, the walls, the columns — they all seem to be covered with diamonds. These are not diamonds, but rather millions of small mirrors. Their edges reflect prism light, throwing out the colors of the rainbow. The resulting effect is spectacular. It leaves visitors speechless.

When the palace was designed, architects ordered mirrors to cover the entrance walls. When the mirrors arrived, they were in pieces — broken during transit. The crates contained countless pieces of shattered mirrors. The first idea was simply to abandon the whole idea.

Then one creative person said, "Let's think again. Maybe it could be more beautiful because it's been broken." The larger pieces were smashed to fit together with the smaller bits in a mosaic labyrinth suffused with rainbow color and brilliance. If the mirrors had not been broken, the effect would have been far less extraordinary.

In *The Secret Garden*, Colin who has been tragically sheltered and made to believe he is very frail and deathly sick discovers otherwise. In a sense, he's a broken person, shattered like the mirror fragments. He is befriended in the secret garden and challenged. His friend doesn't treat him like an invalid and there is a Magic there, Divine Magic.

Colin says in the story that he believes in this Magic (The Big Good Thing) because he once refused to believe in anything or see anything good or believe that Someone, God, cared about him and would show him how to be healed of what hurt him the most. He tells the woman that if he had never been so sick in his spirit he would not know how happy he can be. Colin believes that his inner strength and peace is only possible because he was once broken.

This is the message of Christ. It's the message in the cross of Christ. The horror of suffering is transformed into something staggering in grandeur. That might sound like an impossibility or like a simplistic religious idea. It can take a lifetime to discover this truth. So, for now, just trust that the genuinely beautiful people are usually ones who have been shattered to the core at some point. But in the love of God brokenness is infused with healing. God puts all the pieces together in ways that we'll find surprising.

"There's a healing touch that finds you on the broad highway somewhere to take you high as music flying through the angel's hair . . ." sings Don Henley. This is the Big Good Thing. The Big Good Thing who will use all that hurts you to make you remarkably beautiful. The healing touch will find you, will find all of us. Don't ever stop believing it.

Prayer Starter

Those who look to him are radiant;
their faces are never covered with shame.
This poor man called, and the Lord heard him;
he saved him out of all his troubles.
The angel of the Lord encamps around those who fear him,
and he delivers them.

Psalm 34:5-7

I cannot dance, O Lord, unless you lead me. If you will that I leap joyfully, then you must be the first to dance and sing.
— St. Mechtild of Magdeburg

Soul Writing

Think about some ways you have been broken. Situations in which you have "hit the wall" — discovered that your energy or knowledge or strength just wasn't sufficient. Write about the positive aspects of these experiences. What did you learn? What pleasantly surprised you when you were broken?

45
Going Through the Motions

Something to Think About

My friend Rich had a tradition in his family. It's something they did every Thanksgiving. Something that he found difficult when he was young, but eventually he came to love the tradition.

Each Thanksgiving when the family gathered — uncles and aunts, grandparents and cousins — the families represented brought something to show the others. The object was to represent the thing which that small part of the bigger family was thankful for. Rich remembered when his father's brother brought a baseball mitt because his team was state champion. He thought that was a pretty cool thing to be thankful for.

Life gets complicated, you know that. Tradition is one way to keep our lives ticking along even when we feel empty inside.

But the one he remembers the most was the year his grandmother brought his grandfather's leather work gloves. His grandfather had died that year. She listened while her children and grandchildren told what they were most thankful for and then it was her turn. She reverently pulled the gloves from her sweater pocket and laid them in front of her and said, "I'm thankful for his hands that did good to everyone; he never hurt when it could be avoided; he always touched with love; he worked hard; he used his hands to love. I'm glad to have spent my life safe in the care of his hands."

Making It Mine

Tradition is a way for us to remember. If you've ever lost someone you care about, you know how important remembering can be. Tradition helps us align our lives and stay focused on what matters most. For families it's also a way to remember who we are and what holds us together. As Catholics, our tradition holds us together regardless of our differences under the care of one loving Holy Father, the pope, who keeps us all safely in the hands of God. One way to think about tradition would be to consider it a method by which something that is too important to forget is underlined. We underline by repetition.

If we don't pay attention to tradition, we eventually forget. Anniversaries and birthdays and the sacraments have in common this sense of repetition by celebrating over and over something very important. Tradition does not mean it's always old and tired. Think of it this way: tradition means something has outlasted every human being you'll ever know. Tradition means something is strong enough to resist the ravages of an ever-changing culture. Some have called tradition "going through the motions." But sometimes we go through the motions just so we don't forget the motions. The important motions like prayer. You go through the motions when you are kind to others despite feeling cold inside, or you attend Mass when you think you'd rather be sleeping in. Tradition provides a framework for moving us past our feelings, which are as likely to change as the weather.

Life gets complicated, you know that. Tradition is one way to keep our lives ticking along even when we feel empty inside. Tradition gives us something bigger than ourselves to count on. Tradition keeps us safe in the security of its big, strong hands.

 ## Prayer Starter

To you I call, O Lord my Rock;
do not turn a deaf ear to me.
For if you remain silent,
I will be like those who have gone down to the pit.
The Lord is the strength of his people,
a fortress of salvation for his anointed one.

Psalm 28:1, 8

God, if it's really enough for me to just keep showing up, well, here I am. It's another day, another step, and I'm taking it. Give my steps strength, lift my head, remind me to stay wound.

Soul Writing

What tradition has given you strength when you needed it? What comes to mind when you think of the word "tradition"? Describe tradition in your own words. What Catholic traditions are meaningful for you?

46
How Many Worlds Can You Live In?

Something to Think About

The story of Tarzan has been a favorite of both children and adults for many, many years. The original story, *Tarzan of the Apes* by Edgar Rice Burroughs, is a story of a boy who is raised by apes and in his young adult years discovers his human family. Two worlds, that's how singer-songwriter Phil Collins put it.

The story and the music have resonated with a new generation in Disney's animated feature, but the reason the story resonates remains the same. It is the story of finding yourself. It is the story of belonging. These are so important to what it means to be human that every generation struggles with the same questions. Questions like:

What do I believe about myself?

What do I believe is most important?

When am I most true to myself?

How am I changing and what is the significance of those changes?

How do I remain in my family relationships without losing myself?

Do you ever feel torn between two worlds? Probably often. There's the world of your parents and family, the world where expectations abound. And there's the world of your friends and that whole other set of expectations. You are stretched between these two worlds to the point of snapping sometimes.

How am I changing and what is the significance of those changes?

Making It Mine

Frankie was fifteen when I met her. She was the youngest in a family of three. Her brother, the oldest, was doing a tour for the Army in Germany, and her sister had died in a car accident six months before we met. Frankie worked with me on a teen newspaper. We got to know each other quite well. One day she told me she felt "trapped between the halls of high school and my parents' dreams for me."

She had been close to her sister when they were children, but the teen years hit both of them with the force of an earthquake and their relationship rocked apart. Frankie felt alone and ever since her sister's death the "alone" was bigger than she ever imagined it could be. She was "drowning in loneliness," she told me. She knew her parents loved her, but they were too lost in their grief to see what was happening to Frankie.

Over the next few weeks Frankie and I worked close on a project for the newspaper and we often talked about what first step she could take to feel less alone. Frankie had plenty of ideas so I only listened. She wanted to be a writer. She decided she would become her own best friend. She decided to do it by writing to herself every day. She called it being her own best friend.

That helped a lot. Then she took a second step. She said she would talk to someone who would not die or go away. She made a decision to write to God every day. Shortly after that she told me she was talking to her sister before she went to bed each night. She felt strongly that while death had separated them, nothing could prevent them from being together "spiritually."

She was surprised how what seemed like multiple worlds (parents, friends, the realm her sister had gone to) could come together. Summer ended the newspaper and I lost track of Frankie. Several years later she called me for lunch. She was getting ready to start college, where she would be a journalism major.

"I discovered that the divisions I believed separated me from everyone were mostly in my own mind and spirit. I fragmented my world into little chunks. Do you remember hearing about the Communion of the Saints?" I said I did. "That's how I view the world now. One world with overlapping realms and enchanted places. But it's God's one world and I'm not ever alone."

Prayer Starter

All these people were still living by faith when they died. They did not receive the things promised; they only saw them and welcomed them from a distance. And they admitted that they were aliens and strangers on earth.

Hebrews 11:13

Therefore, since we are surrounded by such a great cloud of witnesses, let us throw off everything that hinders [us] . . . and let us run with perseverance the race marked out for us.

Hebrews 12:1

God, take a look at me and let me feel you are with me. Every day I feel like I lose chunks of myself. Help me hold on, hold me together, and show me what small step I can take to become whole.

Soul Writing

Write a letter to yourself about who you are and what you want for yourself. What do you like about yourself? What are you good at? How is this different from what others think of you? What do you think God thinks of you? Also try writing to someone who has died, someone you care about. Try to imagine how you are connected to all the people in your life and draw a picture of it.

47
Acting Justly When It's Not Easy

Something to Think About

In the fourth century, an Italian monk named Telemachus had the feeling that God was telling him to go to Rome, so he packed his few belongings and went to Rome. As he entered the city he heard loud shouts and saw crowds moving toward the amphitheater. He followed the crowd and climbed to the top of the tiered bleacherlike seating to find a seat. As he settled in and looked down he saw two gladiators begin to fight each other — the entertainment of the day.

How often have you heard people wonder why God doesn't stop horrible things from happening?

He watched horrified as these men, for the sake of entertaining the masses, began to fight to the death. Suddenly, he jumped to his feet and began shouting, "In the name of Christ, stop!" The crowd yelled for him to shut up and sit down. But he shouted even louder and began to make his way down toward the stadium floor all the while shouting, "In the name of Christ, stop!"

When he got to the bottom, he jumped into the arena still shouting for them to cease. One of the gladiators casually flipped his sword at the monk, piercing him fatally. As the monk lay in the dust of the arena he continued to say with his last breath, "In the name of Christ, stop!"

The arena was suddenly quiet. The two gladiators stood looking down at the broken body of the monk, his words echoing in their minds and in the stadium around them. Suddenly, one of them turned away and hurled his sword with a fury, as if he couldn't stand to hold it another minute. The second watched and then did exactly the same thing, silently. The two walked side by side out of the arena. Then the people, one by one and in pairs, got up and left the arena until it was empty. That was the last time gladiators fought in Rome. All because one man had the courage and conviction to say, "In the name of Christ, stop!"

Because of our distance in time from gladiator fights and the atrocities that happened in places like Rome, it is hard to understand what would have made this monk do what he did. It is hard to understand, when the portrayals we've seen of such fights are white-washed with nobility as if such things spoke of a more decent time. There is no noble way to take the life of another human being. It's an old story — I retell it as it was told to me.

 ## Making It Mine

Bud Welch is the father of a twenty-three-year-old woman, Julie Marie Welch, who died with one hundred sixty-seven others in the Oklahoma blast of the Alfred P. Murrah Federal Building on April 19, 1995.

"I was so proud of her," he says. "I bragged on her all the time and it embarrassed her."

For months after the bombing all he wanted was to see the people responsible for the violence pay with their own lives. "I was filled with rage, revenge, and hate," he admits. "I thought, 'Fry 'em.' "

One January day he stood beneath an elm tree across from the bomb site, a place where his daughter used to park her car. He thought about how much this tragedy had changed him. He was smoking three packs of cigarettes a day; he was drinking too much. ". . . and I didn't like myself," he says. "And I thought, after McVeigh and Nichols are tried and executed, how will that help me get through this? And I realized it won't. It won't bring Julie Marie back. Rage, revenge, and hate; that's why Julie Marie is dead."

Bud is Catholic and he spent his life mouthing the words about being against capital punishment. Bud is now fighting against the death penalty. This man who describes himself as filled with rage and hate and wanting the guilty persons to "fry" has met the family of Timothy McVeigh; he has held them while they sob and has promised to fight against the death penalty.

"I go to Mass every week, but I'm not an overly religious person," he says. "I'm not a born-again Christian; I don't even know what that means. I've done some crap in my life. But I've somehow felt closer to God than I ever have since meeting Bill and Jennifer [McVeigh's father and sister]. . . . It brought me so much peace, I can't tell you. . . ."

How often have you heard people wonder why God doesn't stop horrible things from happening? It's a tough question without an answer. The ancient monk Telemachus and Bud Welch are only two examples of people who stopped asking the question and became part of the solution. Justice does not fall out of the sky. It is my responsibility to act justly. It is your responsibility to act justly. That is how justice happens. Capital punishment is not justice — it is vengeance. Justice refuses to enter the cycle of hatred and revenge. That is what it means to turn the other cheek. It is the strong refusal to play the game of striking back.

All the rage, atrocities, and injustice must stop somewhere. Let it begin with me. Let it begin with you.

 ## Prayer Starter

Trust in the Lord and do good;
dwell in the land and enjoy safe pasture.
He will make your righteousness shine like the dawn,
the justice of your cause like the noonday sun.
Be still before the Lord and wait patiently. . . ;
do not fret when men succeed in their ways,
when they carry out their wicked schemes.
For the power of the wicked will be broken. . . .

Psalm 37:3, 6-7, 17a

[God] has showed you . . . what is good.
And what does the Lord require of you?
To act justly and to love mercy
and to walk humbly with your God.

Micah 6:8

Father of us all, the hating obsession must stop. Let it begin now. Let it begin with me. I don't know where to start, so I stand here with an open heart. Show me how to begin. Give me strength. Make me brave.

Soul Writing

Write about an injustice that is important to you. What action can you take against the injustice? How do you understand your responsibility in resisting injustice? What does it mean to love mercy? Do you understand Catholic teaching on capital punishment? What excuses do people make for not acting justly? How would you reply to these excuses?

48
Where the Crowd Leads You

Something to Think About

Author Martha Bolton describes being in a traffic jam. Actually, it appeared that only her lane was jammed. Thousands of cars in front of her and behind her were stopped while the people in the lane beside her whizzed by.

The crowd will take you in the wrong direction. It will get you stuck going nowhere. It will mislead you. It will prevent you from doing what needs doing. Don't trust the crowd.

My first thought was to change lanes. After all, the people in the lane next to me were zooming along, making great time and enjoying the journey. But I figured that since no one else was moving over, they must know something I didn't. Clearly, the majority of the cars on the highway that day were in my lane. They couldn't all be wrong, could they?

So there I sat, along with everyone else, not going anywhere and not doing anything about it but complaining. The solution was right there in front of my eyes — change lanes. But because on one else was doing it, I refused to do it, too.

In life we tend to want to follow the crowd, too. Because there are more people following their own way than are following God's, and they're usually a lot more vocal, we think they must know something we don't. So, we get in line behind them and go nowhere fast.

From *Don't Jump to Conclusions Without a Bungee Cord and Other Wise Advice: Devotions for Teens from the Book of Proverbs* by Martha Bolton

Making It Mine

We were in the Midwest in December and it was cold. About a hundred of us were jammed into a bus and behind us were four or five other busloads of college students, all attending a conference in Urbana, Illinois. I was on staff at the newspaper covering the event. It was early morning and we were getting ready to enter a really large auditorium to pick up our packets and confirm our registrations. The group was lively and excited.

The driver stopped in front of the auditorium and, getting up from his seat, stepped to the middle aisle of the bus and whistled for our attention, which he had no trouble getting. "This is where I'm leaving you off," he explained. "You should line up outside the doors and they'll be opening to let you in for registration in just a couple of minutes." Then he smiled, "It's important that you line up at the doors that have a handle on the outside," he pointed to the east doors, "rather than those that don't have an outside handle," he pointed to the doors on the west side. "Have a great conference and be careful!" he concluded and took his seat.

The young people poured out of the bus and into the crisp morning air, pulling caps over their heads and stomping their feet to keep warm while milling in small groups. Along with a photographer, I was one of the last people out of the bus. He and I were talking when out of the corner of my eye I saw a young man dressed in an army-green coat and carrying an empty backpack head for the wrong door, the doors without outside handles.

And then, as we stood amazed, the entire group, without an exception, moved in the same direction and lined up at the doors without outside handles. With no comment or hesitation they followed the young man blindly to the doors that only seconds before they had been told were the wrong doors!

The crowd will take you in the wrong direction. It will get you stuck going nowhere. It will mislead you. It will prevent you from doing what needs doing. Don't trust the crowd. Be suspicious when you hear the words "everyone" and "everyone knows" or "everyone says."

Prayer Starter

The idols of the nations are silver and gold,
made by the hands of men.
They have mouths, but cannot speak,
eyes, but they cannot see;
they have ears, but cannot hear,
nor is there breath in their mouths.
Those who make them will be like them,
and so will all who trust in them.

Psalm 135:15-18

Know also that wisdom is sweet to your soul;
if you find it, there is a future hope for you,
and your hope will not be cut off.

Proverbs 24:14

God, how do I escape from lining up with all the others even when I suspect it isn't going to get me anywhere? You know how hard it is to be even slightly different from everyone else. So many people don't understand how frightening an idea that is. Make me braver than I know how to be, give me eyes to see the truth and the courage to step out of the crowd.

Soul Writing

Write about a time when you followed the crowd and the result was not what you expected. Why do you (or don't you) follow the crowd? If you were in a courtroom and had to offer evidence that you don't follow the crowd, what would your evidence be? What do you believe happens to those who don't follow the crowd?

49
Don't Kick the Donkey

Something to Think About

The Old Testament (Numbers 22:21-38) tells us the story of the misguided prophet Balaam who was on his way to curse someone when his donkey started talking. Let's back up a bit: the donkey didn't just start talking; she didn't do that until Balaam beat her. Balaam beat her because he was on his way to do something he thought was important and he needed the donkey. The donkey didn't want to go though. She stopped in the middle of the road and would not move.

Balaam is in the middle of beating what is probably the best friend he's got at that point when the donkey yells, "Hey, what are you doing to me? Haven't I been faithful and good to you? Do I deserve this?" (We're paraphrasing, of course.)

If that's not enough to stop a prophet in his tracks, an angel speaks next, saying, "Balaam, you fool, stop beating that animal! Your donkey has just saved your life! If you had continued this idiotic mission of yours, you'd be dead!" The angel left then and Balaam, well, let's hope he carried the donkey all the way home instead of the other way around.

When you've done what you can do to make something happen, and it doesn't happen, chances are there's an angel around keeping you from making a mistake.

Making It Mine

It can be difficult to know when opposition is a test of your courage and perseverance as opposed to when opposition is God's way of stopping you from doing something. But Balaam gives us a good clue. If the situation causes you to become violent, if you are out of control and serving your own selfishness, you're probably on the wrong road.

When you've done what you can do to make something happen, and it doesn't happen, chances are there's an angel around keeping you from making a mistake. Don't beat the thing to death. Don't cripple your friends or make a fool of yourself. Stop. Take a break. Slow down. Think it through again. Maybe it's the path you're taking that is all wrong, or maybe it's your mission.

When the donkey you're riding on won't move another

step, don't kick it. Get off and take a look around. A donkey took Jesus into Jerusalem, where he changed the course of history. Jesus rode the donkey all the way; it didn't stop and even though it was taking him to the toughest moments of his life, Jesus rode it all the way and he didn't beat the donkey.

Often, when you feel there's no way to go on, every possibility is closed, and you have no hope, you're very close to the answer. Look around for an angel, listen for voices you don't expect, and don't go any farther until you know that you know.

 # Prayer Starter

Unless the Lord builds the house,
its builders labor in vain.
Unless the Lord watches over the city,
the watchmen stand guard in vain.

Psalm 127:1

God, it is hard to make decisions that will impact all of my life. I don't want to take it lightly. Help me to know when I have gone as far as I should. My pride keeps me from turning back sometimes. I will need your help if I'm going to do this right.

Soul Writing

What decision are you making now that needs reassessment? What situation most reminds you of a stubborn donkey? Can you think of a situation in which a stubborn donkey might have saved you from harm or a bad choice? What other images from the story of Balaam speak to you?

50
Crosses on a Hill

Something to Think About

Illinois carpenter Greg Zanis was enjoying a family vacation in Florida on April 20, 1999, at 11:20 a.m., when Mark Taylor was shot down by Dylan Kiebold and Eric Harris in what began a horrific shooting spree in Littleton, Colorado, that would stun a country, leave us gasping for air, and wondering how it could have happened.

Immediately after the slaughter, some students at Columbine contacted Zanis, who provides "Crosses for Losses." The students requested fifteen crosses for the lost lives: thirteen victims and two killers who turned their guns on themselves. Zanis immediately left Florida. He worked all night on building the crosses and set out to Littleton where the crosses were set up on a little hill that edged the site of the massacre.

If you've ever taunted other human beings or rejected them for their difference, you're on intimate terms with the beast.

These crosses seemed to capture the deep convulsing grief of America, of teens and parents and teachers and grandparents and friends and siblings. Jutting up in the line of crosses were the crosses of the killers, shrouded in black; at the middle of the line was the cross of the teacher Mr. Sanders, who gave his life to save the kids. This image was cast across a grieving nation and seemed to say it all for us.

Over 125,000 people climbed the hill in the next few days; despite the crowds and nonstop rain, they just kept going to the hill and standing with the crosses, trying to make some sense of it, trying to mark it in time as something we must never forget.

But two of those crosses were like a knife to Brian Rohrbough, whose son, Dan, died outside the cafeteria and whose body was photographed on the sidewalk where he fell. Rohrbough didn't live with his son and didn't know for sure that his son was among the dead until he saw the newspaper photograph. No parent should have to find out his child is dead like that, not ever. Dan Rohrbough was dead there, outside the cafeteria window, for over twenty-four hours before they took his body away.

Brian hated his son's killers having a cross on that hill. At one point Rohrbough and some other victims' relatives could take it no longer. With CNN cameras taping what they were doing, they went to the hill and tore down the killers' crosses and cut them into pieces and threw them in the Dumpster.

Zanis was outraged in Illinois. He said he did not put them up to be a target; he called the action of the grieving relatives "defilement." Rohrbough responded that we don't include Hitler in a monument to the Holocaust. Zanis countered that it was not a monument; rather, it was his way of saying that he cared, and that God loved these people, all of them. He returned the next night, sneaking in to elude the media and in a few moments he had made off with all his crosses. He now takes the originals with him as he talks to youth groups across the country.

 # Making It Mine

What's the truth about this whole situation? Who is right? Who is wrong? Since it was not my teenaged son left dead on a sidewalk for reporters to snap shots of I cannot, will not ever, judge Brian Rohrbough.

But the carpenter Zanis is on to something. Go ahead and cringe at the thought of the killers' crosses side by side on that hill with their victims, but the image contains profound truth. We are living together, you and me, with all the killers, with all the lost, with all that is dark, even within ourselves. If you've ever taunted other human beings or rejected them for their difference, you're on intimate terms with the beast.

And if this terrible beast among us is not somehow included in the redemptive story of the other Cross and Carpenter, then we're all lost and we're all going to end up in Dumpsters. Unless the Cross really does announce the love and pardon of God for all of us, it is not good news for any of us. We desperately need God's love. Yet we grip our hatred with iron fists as if it were a sacred right.

A few days after the Littleton shooting I had lunch with a friend. We discussed how the two killers had been ridiculed and rejected. We speculated at how being always on the outside might drive someone to such a horrific act. I said that even though others might have hurt me at times I could not imagine ever hurting them; the impulse to hurt someone is not one I've ever struggled with.

My good and gentle friend lifted her head. There was something hard in her eyes and she said, "I think I know how they felt. I've imagined hurting the people who made me suffer, who treated me like I was not even human. I don't know why I didn't do it, but I could have." I have been unable to shake the suffering look in the eyes of this adult woman who is one of the best persons I have ever known. She has friends, family, and a husband who has loved her for a very long time. She has work she loves. She attacks life with joy and determination. How could she have been marked for rejection as a teen? How idiotic and blind could those people have been?

The scenario of rejection is replayed time after time in the playgrounds and hallways of schools, in malls, in movie theaters. Someone is taunted. Someone laughs. It isn't harmless fun. It isn't all just a joke. It is evil. It is wrong. It is not much different than murder. It is what breaks person after person.

That doesn't mean the broken person ceases to have responsibilities for his or her choices and actions. The one who pulls the trigger is responsible for the havoc and destruction. Such people rightfully must shoulder the consequences of their actions.

The cruel rejection handed out to the boys who became killers contributed to whatever happened inside those young men. Tormenting others in the name of youthful antics must become as socially unacceptable as sexual abuse, child abuse, or hate crimes. Those who participate in mocking and taunting others need to be held responsible and punished. It doesn't matter if this has been a kind of sport among young people for as long as anyone can remember. It must end. The future depends on it.

Prayer Starter

Dear children, let us not love with words . . . but with actions and in truth. This then is how we know that we belong to the truth, and how we set our hearts at rest. . . .

1 John 3:18

Lord, help me recognize the places in my soul that are closed to the people who are rejected. Help me forgive those who reject me. I will not be defined by them; I will not give to them the power to create me that belongs to you and me. Help me see how I may have become calloused. Lord, have mercy.

Soul Writing

Have you ever participated in mocking or making fun of someone? How do you feel about yourself when you do this? How do you think the object of taunting feels? What makes someone think he or she has the right to treat another human being that way? Write about your experience of rejecting others or being rejected by them.

Theme Index

*Note: The entries in this index are cited
by session (chapter) numbers, not page numbers.*